PLANNING FOR RETIREMENT

PLANNING FOR RETIREMENT

Robert Allen

First published in Great Britain in 2004 by
Virgin Books Ltd
Thames Wharf Studios
Rainville Road
London
W6 9HA

A catalogue record for this book is available from the British Library.

ISBN 07535 0921 0

Typeset by Phoenix Photosetting, Chatham, Kent
Printed and bound in Great Britain by Mackays of Chatham Ltd, Chatham, Kent

CONTENTS

INTRODUCTION: IS IT THE BEGINNING, OR IS IT THE END?

I suppose this book really started a few years ago when I turned 50. After years of working in a highly stressful environment I finally worked up the courage to resign and make a living by writing full time. The work was a bit slow coming at first, but, thanks to some very good friends, I made contacts and soon started to be in demand.

So there I was, feeling happy, fit and young again at the start of a new career. But not everyone saw it that way. Before long the news that I had reached my half century reached the outside world (it's amazing just how many people have your birthdate on a database somewhere). Insurance companies started to get in touch suggesting that I might like to start saving for my funeral – oh, and while I was waiting to die, since I was now too feeble to cause any accidents, they'd give me cheap car insurance. Other people wanted to sell me supplements guaranteed to shrink my ageing prostate, or to interest me in holidays for oldies. The message was clear: I was a dead man walking.

> Inside every old person is a young person saying, 'What the **** happened?'
>
> *Anon.*

Then events took another unexpected turn. My bank sent me one of their occasional magazines which featured an article entitled 'Life Begins at Fifty (and over)'. It told me how the actor Brian Blessed had been on three Everest expeditions since reaching that age, and went on to list a few other energetic oldies. Mick Jagger celebrated his 60th birthday by strutting his hyperactive stuff on the Stones' Forty Licks Tour; actor David Jason became a father at 61; and, as we all know, Michael Douglas married Catherine Zeta Jones at the age of 57 and has since fathered two children. But it's all right for the rich and famous, isn't it? They live in a different world to the rest of us.

It was then that I met Young Arthur.

'It's no good,' my mother had said with a sigh, 'at 82 I'm just too old to keep up the garden on my own. I'll have to advertise for a local lad to help me.'

An ad in the window of the general store brought no replies. Then, late one afternoon a couple of weeks later, the phone rang. It was the owner of the store to say that 'young Arthur' had been in and was interested in the job. Was it still open? Yes, send him round – now!

Young Arthur turned out to be my mother's age at least. The baseball cap worn at a jaunty angle was fooling no one. She was a bit peeved.

'Why do they call you *young* Arthur?' she asked.

'Well, one reason is that my full name's Arthur Young, but if you want to know the other reason you'll have to give me the job,' he replied cryptically.

Having no realistic alternative she agreed, and Arthur started work. He mowed the lawns, straightened the edges, cleared the weeds and reorganised the herbaceous border, then moved on to the fence, which he repaired and repainted before spending some time taking down and removing the old greenhouse. He did everything with vigour and enthusiasm. One day he announced that he needed a week off. He'd bought his wife a new kitchen and had decided to save some money by fitting it himself. Not long after that he bought a new car.

'A bit extravagant at your age, isn't it?' asked my mother with her usual tact and diplomacy.

'Well, I don't know how long I'm going to live, do I?' countered Arthur. 'I'm only 84 and I might have years to go yet.'

After a couple of years' tireless gardening, Arthur had a heart attack. His wife got him to hospital in time and he survived. My mother got a message: 'Don't mess about with that garden yourself – I'll be back.' And he was.

> The value of old age depends upon the person who reaches it. To some men of early performance it is useless. To others, who are late to develop, it just enables them to finish the job.
>
> *Thomas Hardy*

It was while I was pondering the conflicting messages I had received about old age that another thought occurred to me. Who runs this world? It may be the young who form the backbone of the working world, but who is actually in charge? A brief look around the world shows that the president of the USA is in his late fifties, and his main challenger for the job is 60. Tony Blair is over 50 and his main opponent is over 60. Queen Elizabeth II is 78. The Pope is 83. This list is not merely a selection of exceptions to the rule. If you think for a little while you will realise that most of the movers and shakers in this world are in their later years.

So, am I really at the beginning of the end, or is it really true that 50 is the new 30? It seemed to me that the first proposition was just too gloomy to contemplate. After all, I don't *feel* past it, and, at the risk of being called vain, I don't look too bad. More importantly there are things I want to do, places I still want to see. I've never been to New York, Rome or Bombay; I've never experienced the Niagara Falls, or gazed at the Pyramids; I haven't yet flown in a hot-air balloon or been swimming with dolphins; I'd really like to learn Italian, and I want to play the saxophone. In short, I still have a lot of living to do and I'm not about to go quietly.

Everything I know about getting older is either based on my own experience or that of people I know. In preparation for this book I talked to many people about their experiences of ageing and asked what sort of information they would want to pass on to others. I also asked what information they wished they had been given in the past. Many people have been very generous with their advice, and I pass it on with thanks to them. I am particularly grateful to the neighbour who said, 'What on earth do you know about ageing? You're just a lad!'

The trouble with giving advice is that inevitably you have to tell people things they'd rather not know. We all know that we should watch our weight, moderate our drinking and give up smoking, but knowing these things is not the same as doing them. Still, sometimes we all need to be told things that cause us to change our behaviour; the Zen master Dogen once said that good advice should always feel like something that is being forced on you. However, you don't have to try to do it all at once. If you fling yourself into a flurry of self-improvement you are unlikely to keep it up for long. The best way to approach it is to choose one thing at a time and work on it steadily until you achieve your goal. This will give you the impetus you need to go on and try to make other improvements in your life.

> I'm very pleased with each advancing year. It stems back to when I was 40. I was a bit upset about reaching that milestone, but an older friend consoled me: 'Don't complain about growing old – many, many people do not have that privilege.'
>
> *Earl Warren*

You may wonder whether I practise what I preach. I certainly try to, but if it is any consolation I am still not as thin as I should be and, though I attempt to eat a healthy diet, I have many food sins on my conscience. In any case, this book is not intended to turn readers into obsessive health freaks. I can't imagine that a longer lifespan bought at the price of eliminating all the pleasures of life would be an attractive proposition. All the people I came across who were still enjoying an active life in their seventies and eighties did not get to that stage by being overly health conscious but by being full of enthusiasm for life. It doesn't seem to matter much what you are enthusiastic about; the mere fact that you have something that makes you jump out of bed every day eager to get on with your pet project is enough to keep you going in spite of all other difficulties.

A CLASH OF CULTURES

The picture of ageing contained in this book is primarily one shaped by Western society, for once you start writing about age you rapidly come to the conclusion that it's an area where cultural differences are very wide. There is no 'right' way to get older, and it may be that we can learn something from other societies where they do things differently from us.

In the West we have developed an obsession with youth. This is mainly the doing of the boomer generation which was so impatient with the elders in charge when they were young that they rejected the idea that older people might have positive contributions to make. For many years youth represented everything that was good, progressive, interesting and desirable; old age was right out of fashion. Nobody would admit that the lifetime of experience older people had accumulated was worth anything. This rejection masked a secret fear that all young people possess: the old, by their very presence, remind them that their time is limited and that one day they too shall succumb to the ageing process.

> We've put more effort into helping folks reach old age than into helping them enjoy it.
>
> *Frank A. Clark*

This is not how everyone views ageing. In the East, old people are not seen as feeble, worn out, useless and a burden on their family; they are regarded as valuable members of society who have accumulated a lifetime of wisdom which they use for the benefit of their juniors. The interesting thing is that people will live up to the expectations others have of them; because in the East the elders are expected to be wise, virtuous and capable, most of them are.

My own life was influenced by two old ladies I met while I was teaching at a girls' school in Bangkok, Thailand. The first was the grandma of the family I lived with. I was quickly struck by the way she was treated compared with the sort of grandmas I was used to at home. This lady was in every sense the head of the family. If you went away somewhere you always went to her part of the house first to take your leave formally and receive her good wishes for a pleasant journey and a safe return. When you got back you would immediately go to see Grandma and tell her all about your trip. All the affairs of the family were discussed with her as a matter of course. She was asked for her advice, which she gave freely. She would also sanction all family decisions, and when money was to be spent – for example, when part of the family home needed to be extended – she would give the project her consent. Nobody would ever have dreamt of doing anything of importance without Grandma's say-so.

The school where I taught was run by another matriarch. She was well into her seventies but owned two private schools and a construction company, all of which she ran with great energy and efficiency. Her husband had died many years before but she carried on with her business empire with the help of her daughters. Her control was absolute. Each classroom in the school had a loudspeaker through which she would make announcements from time to time. When she did so the teaching would stop and the teachers would wait politely for the headmistress to finish. She also had the classrooms wired for sound and could listen in on your lessons if she wished. Teachers who were heard giving substandard lessons were summoned to her study and shown the error of their ways.

Discipline at the school was quite simple. Naughty girls were sent to stand outside the classroom. The old lady patrolled the corridors regularly, and if she found girls who had been ejected from the class she'd give them a good telling-off. The mere threat of this was quite enough to keep all but the most boisterous pupils under control.

Although the old lady's ideas on education were old-fashioned, no one could deny that the girls left that school well educated and prepared for the outside world. Several of the pupils I knew went on to have impressive careers of their own.

The old lady herself finally retired in her eighties and lived on for a good many years after that. Her place was taken by her daughter, I've been told, who ran the school in the same uncompromising way.

> The heads of strong old age are beautiful beyond all grace of youth.
>
> *Robinson Jeffers*

Some years after I left Thailand one of my former students, now a university undergraduate, came to visit. I was driving into the centre of Cambridge to give her the guided tour when I realised that she was sobbing quietly. I asked her what was the matter, and she said she was so sad because all the old people she saw were on their own. Why didn't we care about our old people? Why didn't their young relatives look after them and accompany them to the shops? She found it incomprehensible that such important family members could be so unloved and unwanted that they would be left to wander around on their own.

It is ironic that now that the boomers are themselves on the brink of old age their views have conveniently changed. Suddenly you hear them saying that '50 is the new 30' or 'people of 50 now think of themselves as 35-and-a-bit'. People now look for examples of oldies who are still active and attractive despite their advanced years. It was revealing, in more than one sense, when Sting, the former lead singer of The Police who had recently celebrated his 50th birthday, pulled off his shirt during an awards ceremony and lounged around showing off his well-developed physique. The message was plain enough: just because someone has reached 50 there is no reason to become old – a sentiment that was not lost on all the fifty somethings who watched the programme.

There is another cultural gulf that is interesting to observe, and that is the difference between attitudes towards ageing in the US and the UK. When Americans write about the elderly they like to describe them as 'seniors' who are enjoying their 'golden years'. There has been much discussion about the exact terminology that should be applied to older people, and words such as 'old' and 'elderly' were quickly ruled out as politically incorrect. Even the term 'senior citizens', which enjoyed a brief period of acceptance, has now given way to 'seniors', which was deemed to have a more positive connotation. When Americans write about age they are mainly obsessed with issues such as diet and exercise that will postpone the inevitable for as long as possible. They maintain an attitude that reeks of positive thinking. The message is, 'I wanna live for ever, and I'm damn well going to.'

However, not all Americans are immune to a certain humour when referring to age. I was recently on a London-bound train that was about to be linked to another unit arriving from King's Lynn. The driver announced that we should sit down because 'during coupling there will be a slight bump'. The operation had just been carried out successfully when an elderly American turned to his wife and said, 'Mary, I haven't felt the earth move like that during coupling for twenty years.'

In the UK, things are very different. The popular magazine that caters for older people is unashamedly called *The Oldie*. The

British attitude to old age rejects political correctness and replaces it with a mordant humour. Older people are quite happy to use apparently derogatory terms in reference to themselves because they see a little self-mockery as a way of dealing with what is really an uncomfortable reality. This attitude was made plain by the couple on a train who passed a huge North London cemetery. It was in the days when smoking was still allowed on trains, and the wife was puffing away happily when her husband turned to her and said, 'Oh, look, darling. There's Marlboro country.'

> You can only perceive real beauty in a person as they get older.
>
> *Anouk Aimee*

But in spite of all the differences there is one thing that remains constant in all cultures, and that is the desire to have a long and happy retirement. And I hope that what follows will help you to achieve this.

In Part One, 'Getting Ready', you will find a discussion of some of the major issues that confront us as we approach retirement, such as attitudes to ageing, and a consideration of what we can do to ensure that we get the best out of our later years. It also covers some purely practical matters such as the type of accommodation we need as we get older. Part Two rejoices in the almost limitless opportunities open to older people in terms of work (both paid and voluntary), education and travel, and Part Three, 'Health and Well-being', deals with things you need to do to stay healthy in order to make the most of those opportunities. It also discusses the most common illnesses which, though frequently suffered by older people, often get ignored until they cause a serious problem.

'The Power of the Mind' explains a number of techniques to help keep your mental abilities – memory, concentration etc. – up to par as you grow older, and 'Family Affairs' looks at the way families change over the years and advises on ways to maintain a good relationship with your grown-up children and grandchildren. Part Six, 'Money, Money, Money', deals with all aspects of finance that will concern you in your retirement, and 'Security Matters' considers ways in which you can safeguard yourself, your house and your hard-earned money. 'The Final Curtain', inevitably, is concerned with death, wills, funerals and bereavement, and gives a step-by-step guide on what you need to do when somebody dies.

Finally, 'The power of the internet' introduces to the world wide web those who have yet to discover its many delights, along with a list of websites (in addition to those mentioned in the course of the text) I know you'll find informative and entertaining.

Throughout the book, too, there are quotations on the subject of old age, as well as potted biographies of famous people who have enjoyed a fruitful seniority, all of which I hope will inspire you. And remember, as the eminently sensible American actress Billie Burke once observed, 'Age is something that doesn't matter, unless you are a cheese.'

One

Getting Ready

WHY PHASE YOURSELF OUT?

WHY HUMANS ARE SPECIAL

When considering the subject of ageing we need to be aware that as humans we possess some unique advantages. The overwhelming majority of creatures born on this planet die before they reach sexual maturity. In human terms, that means they die as children. For example, if you see a pond where thousands of tadpoles are wriggling about, you can be sure that only a tiny number will ever become frogs, and of those an even smaller number will live long enough to breed. Nature uses this huge overproduction of creatures to ensure that enough survive to enable the species to continue.

Humans are not like that. We have developed ways of ensuring that the great majority of our children not only survive to become mature adults but also carry on living for many years after they have finished breeding. In nature, such old age is something so rare as to be hardly known. There are a few creatures, such as the turtle and the whale, that can live long lives, but many more whose lives are brief and are usually terminated when they become a meal for some other creature.

Another strange fact about humans is that we continue to cherish and protect older members of the species even when they are a drain on our resources and are no longer able to contribute much, if anything, to the well-being of the community. You may think that such a state of affairs is quite natural, but in the general scheme of things it is really rather odd. Why do we do it? Some people would give answers touching on morality, or relying on the idea that humans are beings possessing a soul. But the simpler answer is probably that we do it because we can.

> The riders in a race do not stop short when they reach the goal. There is a little finishing canter before coming to a standstill. There is time to hear the kind voice of friends and to say to oneself: 'The work is done.'
>
> *Oliver Wendell Holmes*

Humans have evolved in a very strange way. They are the most curious creatures ever to roam the earth. We want to know absolutely *everything*. We are not merely concerned with matters that have a direct bearing on our society. We don't confine ourselves to problems such as food production or the best ways to protect ourselves from the forces of nature. Instead we investigate millions of ideas for no better reason than that we find them interesting. Humans have studied a plethora of them, from algebra and architecture to zoology and Zoroastrianism. There is nothing we won't poke our noses into. Our only concern is to peer into every corner of our world and try to understand its secrets. We have invented art, drama, philosophy, religion, politics, poetry, quantum mechanics and a million other disciplines just because we are unable to stop ourselves innovating endlessly.

What has this got to do with old age? In the first place, one reason why we struggle to keep the old alive and well looked after is pure self-interest. We fear death and want to put it off for as long as possible; it is therefore clearly in our interest to create a society in which the old are protected and helped to live as long as possible, for one day it will be our turn. The other reason why we preserve the lives of the old is simply because we can. Old age and death are a problem for us, but humans have learnt that they can do just about anything they set their minds to. So if they want to slow down, or even halt, the ageing process, then that is what they will do. We are a long way yet from complete success, but even at this early stage we can appreciate that people are already not only living longer but staying healthy and active for longer.

> You're never too old to become younger.
>
> *Mae West*

But there is something even more important about old age. It is a time of life when we are freed from many of the tasks that keep society running smoothly. It is a time when children have grown up and can care for themselves. Human beings who have little or nothing to do are free to start innovating to their heart's content. Our extended old age has given us precious time in which we are able to indulge in the great human obsession of exploring our world and trying to understand it. Of course, not every older person is going to think great thoughts like Einstein or create paintings like Picasso, but the important thing is that we have the time in which to investigate and ponder. We are given a wonderful opportunity to do all those interesting things that are so important to us as humans.

But just because we have the opportunity it does not mean we will automatically take advantage of it. Traditionally, later life was looked upon as a sort of winding-down process during which we gradually shuffled off our responsibilities and gently whiled away time. There is an old joke that goes, 'A man retires and has all the time in the world. So what do they give him? A gold watch!' A few years prior to his retirement my father's employer offered him a series of seminars entitled 'Phasing Yourself Out'. The aim was to help executives wind down and ease themselves into retired life with as little emotional upheaval as possible. In those days – and here we are speaking about the late seventies – retirement still conjured up images of pipe smoking, carpet slippers, spending more time playing golf or bowls, and pottering about the garden. The main message was that now you had completed your years of work and paid your dues into a pension plan, it was time to sit back and enjoy a peaceful old age.

What a waste! The message going out to older people now is no longer 'Why don't you sit back and take it easy?' but rather 'Why not get moving and do something interesting with your life?' Yes, humans are a very special species. We possess abilities no other creature on earth has ever had and we are able to put them to remarkable uses. So why not use what we have been given and make our lives interesting and full of excitement?

BOOMERS AND THE YOUTH REVOLUTION

This book is concerned with practical advice rather than sociological analysis, but even so it is informative to consider briefly the differences between the boomer generation and its predecessors.

Before World War Two there was no such thing as a 'youth generation'. Young people were regarded merely as junior versions of their elders. There was nothing special about being young; in fact, it was often viewed as a state of immaturity that was to be outgrown as soon as possible. Young men would grow a moustache or start smoking a pipe in an effort to look more like their fathers. Young women adopted the clothes, hair and make-up styles of their mothers in order to be accepted as mature and sensible members of society. Society itself was still hierarchical. People knew their place and, though those in the lower social orders might not have liked it, there was little they could do to change it. On the whole, people deferred to their elders and betters.

But all was not as peaceful as it might have appeared. There were plenty of people who felt that they deserved a greater say in the way society was run. The war provided the enormous shock that allowed society to be changed radically. Returning servicemen were determined that there should be a new sort of society in which wealth and opportunities were more fairly distributed. The British General Election of 1945 produced a convincing victory for the Labour Party, which signalled that people were no longer willing to accept the old system in which the mass of the public meekly submitted to the will of their 'superiors'.

This change was remarkable in itself, but what was to come was even more mind-boggling because it was something that had never happened before in the entire history of the world. The first signs of change emerged in the US in the 1950s. Young people started to embrace not only rock 'n' roll but also new styles of clothing and speech that were, for once, their own and owed nothing to the styles favoured by their parents. Looked at from the perspective of the twenty-first century it may be hard to see what all the fuss was about, but at the time this departure from the norms of society was seen as not only revolutionary but dangerous. Parents, teachers, religious leaders and politicians alike were deeply disturbed by what they perceived as a society going crazy. But the roars of moral outrage had quite the opposite effect from the one intended. Young people were delighted to have a culture of their own that cocked a snook at the world order their parents tried to force on them.

> There was no respect for youth when I was young, and now
> that I am old, there is no respect for age. I missed it
> coming and going.
>
> *J. B. Priestley*

It is doubtful that anyone at the time really understood the enormity of what was happening. Superficially, the fuss was all about clothing, music and other fairly trivial matters. But the rift went much deeper than that. It was about young people no longer being willing to obey unreservedly their elders and rejecting the sort of society the older generation represented.

Communication was slower in those days, but it wasn't long before such attitudes were being exported via films and TV across the Atlantic, and they were soon being copied, to the utter horror of all adults, both in the UK and Europe. The enthusiasm with which the new culture was seized upon showed that it had touched a nerve with young people everywhere. Their parents had wanted to see changes in society but had had no desire for a revolution. But whether they liked it or not, a revolution was what they were about to get.

It wasn't long before youngsters of all Western nations started to think of themselves as 'teenagers', a new term that inspired those it applied to as much as it disgusted their parents. In Britain, the aping of American youth led eventually to the establishment of homegrown youth styles. Music was revolutionised by the Beatles, the Rolling Stones and endless other new pop groups. For the first time ever young people had produced a culture that was utterly different from that of their parents, whom they now viewed as being hopelessly square.

The Rolling Stones

There are many examples that typify the new oldies, but one of the most significant must be the Rolling Stones, who in 2003 embarked on their Forty Licks Tour. Here was a group that had once been the archetypal teenage rebels. They'd done sex, drugs and rock 'n' roll with a vengeance and had been lambasted by all the pillars of the establishment many times over. Now, in their sixties, they were performing on a huge world tour. Anyone who has ever seen the Stones on stage will know just how much sheer physical effort goes into everything they do. Did they look like a bunch of sad old men trying pathetically to hang on to their youth? No way! They performed with as much vigour as ever and were greeted with adulation not just by their former fans but also by the children of those fans. The final irony, of course, was when Mick Jagger was given a knighthood (much to Keith Richards' disgust). Could anyone 30 or 40 years ago have imagined that one of the bad boys of rock would end up as an establishment figure?

It was by no means a peaceful process. Adults were quick to recognise the challenge to their power and tried hard to stamp it out. Schools became a battleground where teenagers would try to adopt the fashion styles that appealed to them in spite of vigorous opposition from those in authority. Boys with long hair and girls with short skirts were seen as undermining the authority of teachers, yet it was impossible to eradicate such challenges. There was a limit to what teachers were allowed to do to rebellious pupils, and slowly but surely teenagers pushed the limits of acceptable behaviour further and further. Only in the communist countries of Eastern Europe was it possible to use really draconian measures to keep the young under control.

The adults of that time took comfort in the fact that the young generation would eventually have to get jobs and acquire mortgages and children – in short, be forced to knuckle down by the sheer pressure of responsibility. These things did happen, but they left the boomer generation to a large extent unchanged. The boomers had certain articles of faith they were unwilling to abandon. They rejected almost everything previous generations had felt was sacrosanct. They pushed for a radical rethink on the way in which the world was being run. They regarded anyone over the age of 30 as being hopelessly out of touch and quite unable to relate to the modern world.

Life can only be understood backwards, but it must be lived forwards.

Soren Kierkegaard

The Vietnam War was the great battleground. The issue of drafting turned the rift between young and old into an unbridgeable chasm. For older Americans who had fought in World War Two and the Korean War, this new war was just as important. Many saw it as an essential part of the fight against world communism, a time when the youngsters could repay the debt they owed to the veterans of earlier conflicts. The young did not see it that way at all. They were searching for a society that was based on peace and love. Hippies walked around with flowers in their hair and a hope for a better future in their hearts. Not only did they not want to die in some foreign jungle, they fundamentally disagreed with the policies of those who would send them there. The peace movement became an international affair and was embraced even in countries such as Great Britain where the government was adamantly opposed to sending our young men to fight in Vietnam.

The rift between young and old now became truly serious, and it became linked to a whole range of other issues such as racial equality and women's rights. Had America been able to win in Vietnam it is just possible that the youth revolution might have fizzled out, but when the most powerful nation on earth was subjected to a humiliating defeat it became clear that the world had changed permanently.

It has to be said that much of the so-called youth revolution was silly and badly thought out. There was a prolonged period during the late 1960s and early 70s when everything seemed in turmoil; while people knew the sort of society they didn't want, they were much vaguer about what they did want and how they could get it. Many of the ideas that were spawned in that era have long since found their way to the rubbish heap of history.

> The old age of an eagle is better than the youth of a sparrow.
>
> *Anon.*

Nonetheless, something odd had happened. As the boomers grew older, they retained the desire to be young. At first sight this may seem like a pathetic Peter Pannish desire to hang on to one's youth. But it was rather more than that. The boomers were aware that not only did they not feel old, they remained in better shape than their forebears had done. The idea that at a certain age one should start to grow old gracefully just did not appeal to them. They still associated the whole idea of being old with the attitudes their parents had held, which they had so forcefully rejected. And so far they had led fortunate lives. With the exception of those unfortunate enough to have been sent to fight in Vietnam, they had not suffered a cataclysmic war the way their parents had, and they found themselves living in the most prosperous society ever known to man. Why should they give all this up and settle for a quiet old age? Those who had reached 50, far from winding down, were keen to keep going and enjoy all the other things life had to offer. There was no question whatever of phasing themselves out – they were preparing to have a second go at life.

The boomers found that they had much more in common with their children than they'd ever had with their parents. Although there were the usual tensions, the generation gap was far narrower than it had ever been before. The boomers were not horrified by their kids' appearance, music or lifestyle. Indeed, they actually approved of much that their kids were doing. Music that had been familiar in the 1970s was recycled, as were clothing fashions. Who would ever have thought that those flared jeans would come back? The boomers have always been a fashion-conscious generation. For them, fashion was not just about looking good, it was also a way of signalling to the older generation that they were no longer willing to accept the way society had been run in the past. Their long hair and weird psychedelic clothes signalled a complete break with the dull, conformist, snobbish society of their elders.

As they grew older, the boomers inevitably changed in some ways, but they never turned into clones of the previous generation. The values and styles they had invented for themselves still influenced their behaviour. You can look at any group of businessmen these days and you'll find that few of them now sport the traditional grey suit and sombre tie, and those who do probably get into jeans and a T-shirt at the weekend. Yet they haven't mellowed much in other areas. Their dislike of authority and their desire to reshape the world in a way that suits them remains as strong as ever.

Having taken on the older generation and won, they were now ready to take on the idea of old age and change that. The people who had spent their whole lives tearing down an old system and trying to build a new one now faced their biggest challenge – to make their own old age a pleasant and fulfilling experience. This idea appealed not just to the boomers themselves but to the new younger generation, who looked at the road ahead and felt that they too would never want to lose the enthusiasm and mental vigour of youth.

> I will never give in to old age until I become old.
>
> *Tina Turner*

All the signs so far are good. Already there are many older people who simply refuse to behave as if they are 'old'. They may have aged a bit in body, but the mind is still fully alive and eager to grab as much life as possible while the going is good.

REINVENTING YOURSELF

Who do you think you are? We all identify ourselves with a role of some sort. Many people think of themselves in terms of the job they do. For many years I was responsible for publishing the year-book of a well-known club. Each member was allowed to contribute a personal message of twenty words. It was quite astonishing that a very high proportion of the contributors chose to talk solely about the work they did. This was a social organisation where people went to relax outside working hours, yet it was obvious just how many people felt that who they were in their working hours was the most important thing about them.

Naturally, not everyone feels that their identity depends on their role at work. Others might think of themselves primarily as parents, sportsmen, musicians, artists, or one of many other roles. How we choose to see ourselves is very important to us. It is not just a mask we choose to wear, it is the very essence of who we think we are. Our role is something we have freely chosen as being the most attractive and important of all the options available to us. Its part in our life is hard to overestimate.

Take the case of someone who is the managing director of a business enterprise. His role is to be the boss. He is treated with respect and, if he's a good boss, some affection. He can hire and fire people, so he is also feared to some extent. He not only feels that he is in control of the organisation but that the welfare of the employees depends heavily on his ability to make the right business decisions. Because he carries so much responsibility he is very well paid and enjoys a luxurious lifestyle. Even when he is outside the working environment he has a sense of self-worth based on his boss persona. Even when he is dealing with situations where his work role is not really relevant he feels confident and in control because he still feels himself to be in charge.

> A person is always startled when he hears himself
> seriously called an old man for the first time.
>
> *Oliver Wendell Holmes*

What happens to such a person when he retires? From one day to the next his status has gone. Now, even if he were to revisit his old company he would not enjoy the automatic deference that was his due when he was working. This loss of status can have serious consequences. For maybe several decades our man has thought of himself as the head honcho, and now that that is over he may suddenly feel worthless. He is used to having a highly structured day during which his valuable time was spent dealing with numerous important matters. But now he has nothing to do. He can do whatever he wants, of course, but nothing will give him the same good feeling he had when he was in charge of a company. In these circumstances he may start to feel listless. If this mood continues it may well turn into a clinical depression.

It isn't just powerful businessmen who feel this way. All sorts of people find that as they age they are no longer required to perform the same roles as before. For example, parents find that when their children leave home they no longer need or want constant help in their lives. Some parents buy a pet as a sort of substitute child, but, of course, owning a dog is not and never can be the same as having children.

Rolf Harris

If you are 30 or more you will remember Rolf Harris as the perky young Australian who drew cartoons while telling funny stories. For most of his career he was a provider of light entertainment. He could paint, sing a bit, and tell amusing stories. But it was not until he reached the age of 63 that his biggest breakthrough happened. He was asked to host a short run of a new BBC series called *Animal Hospital*, and to his amazement and that of all the others involved, the programme was an overnight hit. Nine million people were watching regularly, and for some shows the figure reached eleven million. The series that had been intended to run for a week actually ran for ten years. Impressive though that is, it is not the end of the story.

Harris had always been known for his ability to produce amusing paintings but no one had ever taken his artistic aspirations very seriously. Now, because of his renewed popularity, he was asked to present a show entitled *Rolf on Art*. Cynics thought that the show was no more than a catch-penny exercise to cash in on the appeal of a famous face. To their surprise, it turned out that Harris did know about art and was a very gifted painter. Eventually his paintings were exhibited in London's National Gallery. Now in his seventies he is more popular than ever, and it looks as though his career is far from over.

Accepting the loss of one role and searching for another is no easy matter. The period of transition can be extremely painful and confusing. When you have spent many years thinking of yourself in a certain way it can be hard to change that view and find another. Accepting that circumstances have altered and that your role needs to move with them can be unsettling.

The very worst way to handle this situation is to try to cling on to your former role. It is not unusual to come across elderly employees in a company who were once important members of the management and have managed to wangle themselves a job as a 'consultant'. They wander around the building chatting to the employees and telling tales of the good old days. If they are lucky, the younger staff will treat them with a sort of amused tolerance, but often they are seen as ancient bores who are to be avoided at all costs. Now, what sort of life is that?

Similarly, you come across parents who 'help' their grown children by interfering in their lives all the time. This is just a recipe for disaster. Far from maintaining a good relationship with the children it serves only to exasperate them and drive them away.

> To be 70 years young is sometimes far more cheerful and hopeful than to be 40 years old.
>
> *Oliver Wendell Holmes*

However difficult it may be, you simply have to find a new role – but how? The first thing to do is to establish what role you have been playing and to consider whether it will change as you get older. Because playing a role is something we do quite naturally we are not always conscious that we are doing it. We sometimes identify so closely with a role that we simply think of it as 'me'. The questionnaire below should help you identify your role so that you have a chance of anticipating difficulties before they arise. There are no right or wrong answers; the sole purpose of the questions is to get you thinking and help you understand which role you have been playing and how it might change in the future.

WHO DO YOU THINK YOU ARE, AND WHO DO YOU WANT TO BE?

1. What activity takes up most of your time?
2. Is this activity pleasurable or is it something you are forced to do?
3. If you were no longer able to take part in this activity would you be happy or sad?
4. Which activities give you the most pleasure?
5. Which people depend on you most?
6. Is it important to you that people depend on you?
7. Will this dependency change over time?
8. If the answer to question 7 was 'yes', do you see the change as being for better or worse?
9. On a scale of 1 to 10, how important is work in your life?
10. On a scale of 1 to 10, how important are your children in your life?
11. On a scale of 1 to 10, how important are friends in your life?
12. On a scale of 1 to 10, how important are hobbies and other leisure activities in your life?
13. What proportion of your free time do you spend with your partner?
14. Do you value time spent away from the family?
15. Do you look forward to retirement or is it something you dread?
16. When the children leave home, will you be glad to get your life back or will you feel a sense of loss at their departure?
17. When you retire, will you miss a sense of being in control?
18. Will retirement have a negative or positive effect on your social life?
19. When you have nothing to do all day, will you know how to fill your time and keep boredom at bay?
20. Can you envisage a new role that you would like to fill?

A SENSE OF PURPOSE

Nowadays, retirement often starts with what is called 'the honeymoon', and it may last anywhere from a couple of months to a year or more. The honeymoon is that period during which the recently retired feel that they have been given an extended holiday. They start off by doing all the things they have ever wanted to do with great enthusiasm. If they were used to playing golf once a week, they now play as often as they wish. If they could only find time for one foreign holiday a year, they now have two or three. Then there are all those pet projects they have always wanted to get on with – redecorating the house, reading loads of books for which they had never found time before, setting up a workshop for their hobbies, landscaping the garden.

However, as we all know, a holiday can't last for ever. The things you do on holiday are enjoyable precisely because they are a break from routine. If they actually *become* your routine you will soon find that you get bored. It will eventually dawn on you that this is not the holiday you thought it was; it is actually the beginning of the rest of your life. It is when this thought arises that people tend to become depressed. Suddenly they are faced with many years stretching out before them and no real idea of how to spend their time. If no answer is found to this problem it can lead to a major identity crisis. In order to replace the sense of identity we had when we were younger we need to consider a number of factors:

- status;
- having goals;
- a need to be creative;
- the necessity for structure;
- the need for action;
- a desire for mental stimulation;
- the need to earn money;
- the need for a social network;
- the need for excitement.

Let's consider these one by one.

STATUS

Everybody has the need to be a 'somebody'. This needn't mean that you want to be a person of huge importance, but you do need to feel valued. My father had been retired for a year and was at rather a low ebb when unexpectedly his old employers phoned to ask if he would be able to take on some part-time consultancy work. He was up the stairs, into his business suit and out of the door in no time. Suddenly he had ceased to be a bored and frustrated old man and had once again become somebody of value. After a few years of part-time work he found that he had grown used to the idea of being retired and was able to leave his job and spend the rest of his life enjoying his hobbies. It doesn't much matter what you do in retirement, but there must be something that makes you continue to feel that you have status.

HAVING GOALS

Throughout our lives we have goals set for us by parents, teachers and employers. We also set goals for ourselves. We decide that we want a better job, a bigger house or a newer car. Once you retire, setting yourself goals can become more difficult. A lot of the situations that once inspired us are no longer available. But it is important to replace them. The effort involved in attaining our goals is therapeutic, so think of things you intend to strive for. Having goals will help you get out of bed every day.

CREATIVITY

Creativity is a uniquely human urge. The constant desire to come up with new ideas is what has made us such a productive species. We can be creative in many ways, but if your creativity was connected to your employment it may be that your opportunities to produce ideas will be lost once you retire. If so, you need to find a replacement. Creativity takes many forms. People usually think of it in connection with artistic, musical or literary activities, but they are only a few areas where the creative urge can be satisfied. It can also be sated in areas as diverse as problem solving, scientific investigation and cookery. The creative urge is largely the province of the unconscious mind, and for reasons we do not fully understand this activity has a very powerful and positive effect on our mental health. Whatever you decide to do in retirement you would be well advised to find some sort of creative work to stimulate you.

> I have enjoyed greatly the second blooming that comes
> when you finish the life of the emotions and of personal
> relations; and suddenly find – at the age of 50, say – that a
> whole new life has opened before you, filled with things you
> can think about, study, or read about . . . It is as if a fresh
> sap of ideas and thoughts was rising in you.
>
> *Agatha Christie*

STRUCTURE

When we are working it is easy to structure our time. We know
that we have to go to our place of work, hold meetings, answer
correspondence, make decisions and then, at a fixed time, we go
home where we do household chores, relax and socialise. Often
our lives are so full of activity that we have to keep a diary just to
keep track of all the things we have to do. Retirement takes that
structure away from us. Suddenly we do not have to get up at any
specific time and we have far fewer duties to perform. If the children have left home then we don't have to worry about getting
them organised. This lack of structure can be very bewildering.
After years of hectic activity suddenly there is an ocean of time in
which you can do what you like. In the past the time you devoted
to relaxation and hobbies was pleasant precisely because it was a
break from work; now you can relax all you like, but because there
are no set limits the things you used to enjoy are just not as much
fun. So it is important to structure your day. Don't just do things
when you get round to them; make sure you have a routine that
prevents you from just drifting and losing your motivation.

ACTION

You know that feeling you get on a wet Sunday afternoon in mid-
winter? The lack of activity makes you bored, and the boredom
makes you listless. Eventually you get so bored that you fall
asleep, and when you wake up you feel no better. People *need*
activity. It is not important what you do, but it must be something
that involves physical work. You don't have to do anything too
exhausting – this is not about taking exercise – but you do need to
do something that gets you up out of your chair and gives you a
reason to move about for a while.

> The old horse in the stable still wants to run.
> *Chinese saying*

MENTAL STIMULATION

There is medical evidence that people who keep an active mind are much less likely to suffer from dementia as they grow older. Your brain works on the same principle as the body – use it or lose it. If you have been in the habit of being mentally active then you need to keep it up. If you haven't had much opportunity to expand your mental horizons, don't worry – it is never too late to start. Puzzles, quizzes, crosswords and jigsaws are all excellent for keeping the mind alert. Playing difficult games such as chess or bridge is another method for keeping the little grey cells fully occupied. If you use the internet you'll be able to find all sorts of people all over the world who share your interests and are keen to meet up online to discuss them. You should especially work on improving your memory (see page 148). It is by no means inevitable that memory fades as we get older. If you work at it, most people will be able to retain their powers of memory for life.

EARNING MONEY

We need money to live, but there is more to it than that. Earning money is also associated with feelings of self-worth. We have all been taught from our youth that earning a living is one of our most important goals, and for that reason our earning capacity is strongly connected to whether or not we feel valued by our family, friends and neighbours. It is very common for people who lose a job also to lose their self-respect and feel that they have become worthless because of their inability to provide an income for their family. Some retired people with good pensions are fortunate enough not to need money in order to live comfortably, but that does not mean that they are not still motivated by the desire to earn. If you feel strongly that your earning power is involved in your feelings of self-worth then you should not shun work just because you don't need the money. Take on some paid work again and your mental health will be much improved by the feeling that you are earning a living (see 'Work' on page 62).

> Age is only a number, a cipher for the records. A man can't retire his experience. He must use it. Experience achieves more with less energy and time.
>
> *Bernard Baruch*

SOCIAL NETWORK

For many of us, work provides opportunities for socialising. Plenty of people make friends with their work colleagues and enjoy leisure time with them. Once you stop work it is unlikely that such friendships will last long. It is the shared experience of the workplace that has been holding you together, and once that is lost it's sometimes hard to find enough things to make the friendship interesting. There are other social networks many of us belong to that break down in later years. If you have children, it is likely that some of their friends' parents are also your friends, but once the kids have left home the reason for your friendship may become weaker. It is therefore important to make an effort to find new groups to join. Clubs, classes, places of worship and the organisation of local activities all provide a chance for you to strike up new acquaintances to replace those you have lost.

EXCITEMENT

When we are young, excitement is not hard to find. Just visit a theme park and you will see hundreds of people taking white-knuckle rides and screaming with a mixture of pleasure and terror. But as we grow older, some of those things no longer hold the same attraction, and others we are no longer physically able to participate in. The need for excitement never really leaves us, and it is a good idea to look for activities that you still find thrilling. A surprise from time to time or an activity that contains an element of risk helps to stave off boredom and keep the mind invigorated.

> We don't grow older, we grow riper.
>
> *Pablo Picasso*

REDRAWING YOUR MAP

Psychologists place a lot of emphasis on our 'mind map', which is simply our view of how the world is. All sorts of things get included on the map such as your relations with friends and family, religious and political opinions, preferences, hopes, fears and aspirations. The question we must now ask is, are you the sort of person who is constantly redrawing that map or did you decide on a final version by the time you reached early middle age? Some people are happy to settle into a comfortable rut and see no reason ever to change. They have decided all the major issues in their life once and for all. This feeling of certainty gives them security.

However, refusing to change your mental map has a downside. The only way we continue to grow, to learn and to profit from new experiences is by being open to change and constantly revising our mental map to take account of new experiences. In fact, this is how real maps are made. There can never be a final version because the landscape is constantly in flux. Cartographers spend a large proportion of their time collecting new data in preparation for the next edition of a map, and as soon as that is published the process of updating begins all over again.

> You only hurt yourself when you're not expanding and growing. Many people can't stand the thought of ageing, but it's the crystallised thought patterns and inflexible mind-sets that age people before their time. You can break through and challenge your crystallised patterns and mind-sets. That's what evolution and the expansion of love are really about.
> *Sara Paddison*, The Hidden Power of the Heart

If you want to enjoy good mental health and an active life in your later years it is essential that you are able periodically to revise your map. Failure to do so will mean that you get stuck in a mental cul-de-sac where you will stagnate. It is quite easy as we get older to stick to what is familiar, safe and known and to ignore or reject anything that smacks of change. But it is precisely the mental effort involved in revising our mental map that keeps us young. The sort of older people who constantly make unflattering comparisons between today's world and that of their youth are not only making themselves unpopular with youngsters, they are also depriving themselves of new, interesting and exciting developments.

The modern world is so complex and moves so fast that many people, not just older ones, find it confusing and sometimes quite scary. It is essential that we screw up the courage to embrace change. To turn our backs on the world of today and try to live in some sort of retro-world of our own devising is foolish.

Bruce Forsyth

In the mid-1950s a TV show called *Sunday Night at the London Palladium* first brought Bruce Forsyth to national attention, and he has been on our screens ever since. During his career he has hosted many game shows (most notably *The Generation Game*), featured in films, and appeared as a guest on more shows than you can count. His trademark catchphrases, 'Nice to see you, to see you nice' and 'Didn't he do well?', are familiar to just about every one of us. He is now in his seventies but is still regularly seen on TV. His act is as energetic as ever and he shows no signs of slowing down, giving up or refusing to try new things. In a recent interview for BBC Radio 2 he made it quite clear that he was enjoying performing as much as ever and had no plans to retire.

To keep your mental map open to change, the main quality you need is curiosity. Thanks to modern communications we now have more information at our fingertips about the world around us than any generation before us. Every day we are bombarded with news from all over the world. Information that would at one time have taken weeks or months to reach us is now transmitted in seconds. It is quite normal now for people to carry on real-time conversations with friends or colleagues in far-flung corners of the earth.

It is just not possible to absorb everything that reaches us, but we don't have to. We can select what we want to know and ignore the rest.

Furthermore, in a world where international travel has become commonplace we are now in a position to do something that would have been unthinkable a generation ago: we can go and see these far-off places for ourselves (see 'Travel' on page 84).

What really matters is not just that we are able to access a lot of information. The important thing is to plot it on our mind maps and be willing to allow this information to change us and the way we think about our lives. There is a Chinese saying that goes, 'What does a frog in a well know of the sea?' People who lead little lives and never venture outside territory that is safe and known will never be able to grow, but those who open themselves up to new ideas and experiences will be greatly enriched.

It is the willingness to keep on growing in knowledge and understanding that helps to keep us young. Humans are a naturally curious species, and a thirst for new information is a strong element in our character. As the years go by, however, it is easy to let that thirst for knowledge dry up. Some older people start to feel that the modern world is no longer theirs but belongs to the younger generation. They deliberately distance themselves from anything they regard as newfangled and convince themselves that they couldn't possibly understand it. By doing this they are depriving themselves of the chance to remain involved in the world and to continue to grow and develop.

> You can judge your age by the amount of pain you feel when you come in contact with a new idea.
>
> *Pearl S. Buck*

Think, for example, of all the truly amazing things that are being discovered in the world of science. You don't have to be a scientist to get at least a basic understanding of them. Magazines such as *Focus*, *New Scientist* and *Scientific American* publish summaries of the most exciting recent developments in language that is completely accessible to the interested amateur (see website list in 'The power of the internet' on page 231). If science isn't your thing, then there are many other areas to explore. Our world is literally buzzing with information, and much of it is of real interest to those who take the trouble to find it.

The more you open your mind to new developments the more exciting the world seems. I will never forget when my father-in-law, who was over 70 at the time and a card-carrying technophobe, bought himself a computer. We were amazed that within a very short time he was using it for word processing, and not long after that he introduced himself to the delights of email and the internet. When he found that you could actually buy tickets for journeys or theatre performances online, his enthusiasm knew no bounds.

Older people who retain their enthusiasm and curiosity can be a delight. An old friend who works at a scientific department at Cambridge University was recently invited to the departmental barbecue. This was the first such occasion she had attended, and, feeling a bit apprehensive, she invited me to go along and provide moral support. To be honest, I was a bit wary of going myself. I had visions of being bored to death by a crowd of aged dons who could talk about nothing but their own research. But I could not have been more wrong. Some of the scientists were well beyond 50 and a few were the wrong side of 70, but they were a lively and interesting bunch full of enthusiasm for a wide variety of subjects and able to talk knowledgeably about current affairs, books, music and a host of other subjects. What had promised to be a dull afternoon turned out to be one full of interest and amusement.

> I am an old man, but in many senses a very young man.
> And this is what I want you to be, young, young all your life.
> *Pablo Casals*

So, how does one go about drawing up a mind map? The mind map is usually just a figure of speech that helps us understand the way we think about ourselves, but it is possible to draw one up if you want to try the mind-mapping technique taught by Tony Buzan.

- Get hold of a large sheet of paper – the sort of lining paper that decorators use is cheap and useful for this purpose.

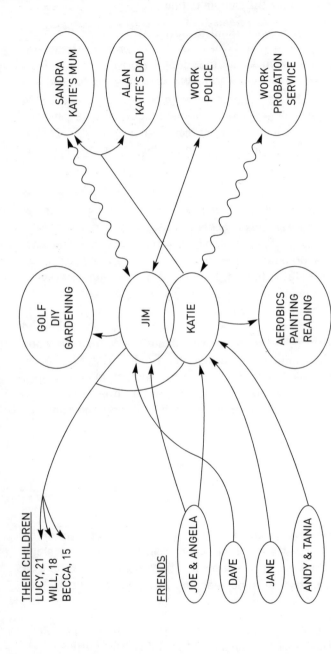

This is an elementary mind map for Jim and his wife Katie. It shows their relationships to family, friends, children, work, and outside interests. A jagged line indicates a problematic relationship (you can see that Jim doesn't hit it off with Katie's mum and Katie is unhappy about her career). The map can be expanded as much as you wish. As it gets more complicated, you may have to redraw it and introduce coloured arrows to keep the relationships clear. Try a map of your own life and see what it tells you about the way you perceive your relationships.

- Start by putting yourself in the centre of the map and then begin to add in all the things that make up your life. It helps if you make the map as visually interesting as possible by adding drawings and symbols as well as text. You can include relatives, friends, interests, work, hobbies, religion, politics and so on.
- Next, draw connections between all these factors. Eventually you will create a map that shows all aspects of your life and the status you attach to them, i.e., those things that are really important, those that are there simply out of habit, and those that you have always intended to change but have never got round to doing so. Try it, and you will be amazed just how much it can teach you about your life and the way it is organised.

For more information about mind mapping, you can look at Tony Buzan's *How to Mind Map: The Ultimate Thinking Tool That Will Change Your Life* (HarperCollins), or *The Mind Map Book: Radiant Thinking – Major Evolution in Human Thought* (BBC).

ATTITUDES TO AGEING

People are obsessed by age. The news media regularly mention someone's age regardless of whether it is relevant to the story or not. It is easy to blame the media for this fixation, but it would be unfair because all they are doing is reflecting the interest the general public has. People are forever discussing how old so-and-so is and whether he/she looks good or bad for his/her age.

It is important as you get older not to become intimidated by numbers. Sadly, there are still far too many people who look no further than a person's age before making judgements about how they should behave and what they might be capable of doing. Much of the time these attitudes are hidden behind supposedly humorous remarks that are intended to keep older people in their place. People who would never dream of making racist or sexist jokes will quite happily describe someone in later life as being 'ready for a bus pass' or 'in need of a Zimmer frame'. These attitudes are slowly being worn away, but there is a long way to go before older people get the sort of respect they deserve.

> I'm not interested in age. People who tell me their age are silly. You're as old as you feel.
>
> *Elizabeth Arden*

The truth is that, thanks to better medical care and healthier lifestyles, there are now many people who would once have been 'old' who are now physically and mentally middle-aged. My in-laws, for example, are both in their mid-seventies but are quite happy to hike fifteen miles a day in the mountains. I always draw some harmless amusement from watching them overtake people half their age who are busy trying to catch their breath after the first climb of the day.

It is not unusual to hear old people say, 'It's only the outside that changes; on the inside, I feel just like I used to.' Of course, there are physical changes that make life a bit harder. People find that they are not as agile as they once were, some might need glasses, others may find they are getting a bit hard of hearing. But the enthusiasm that lies inside the mind can remain undimmed.

It is remarkable just how much enjoyment people can get from life even when the body is in a state of decline. The most lively and enthusiastic lady I ever met was one of my mother's friends – let's call her Iris. I'd known her when she was in her fifties and in those days she used to be involved in all sorts of village activities, from running the baby clinic to organising trips for the elderly. As she got old herself she remained as active as ever. Eventually she had a brush with cancer, as well as suffering from a nagging heart condition and arthritis that destroyed both her hip joints. Now, that would be enough to make most of us lose some of our zest for life, but if it bothered Iris, she never let it show. She was a regular on all the elderly people's outings and continued to run her baby-weighing sessions until she was well over 80. Eventually her various ailments caught up with her, but her son told me her last words were quite typical of her: 'Don't worry, I'll be all right in a minute.'

> We do not grow absolutely, chronologically. We grow sometimes in one dimension, and not in another; unevenly. We grow partially. We are relative. We are mature in one realm, childish in another. The past, present and future mingle and pull us backward, forward, or fix us in the present. We are made up of layers, cells, constellations.
>
> *Anais Nin*

It is important, like Iris, to learn to think of yourself not in terms of chronological age but in terms of what you are still capable of doing. This is far more revealing than how many birthday-cake candles you have to blow out. Because the phenomenon of a whole generation of sprightly, fit and mentally alert older people is a new one, the idea hasn't quite sunk in yet and people are unwilling to give up the idea of the elderly as being senile, frail and incompetent. But, just as prejudice against women, gays, ethnic minorities and the disabled has been made unacceptable in recent times, so will prejudice against the elderly. Every older person who achieves things that would have seemed impossible a generation ago helps to consign age prejudice to the rubbish heap of history.

PANIC STATIONS

One of the secrets of growing old well is to have the right attitude. This is more difficult than it sounds. People have many ways of dealing with the discovery that they have reached the third phase of their life. Some slip into it quite comfortably – we all know people who seem to have been old for years – but many of us find the onset of later life disturbing, and for a few it is deeply traumatic. There are many ways of handling the transition, some of them perfectly sensible, others less so. A few are plainly disastrous.

Men often suffer their first age-related panic when they start to go grey and/or lose their hair. You don't have to be very old for this to happen, but at any age it is a powerful reminder that your youth is not a permanent state. So what do you do? Here are some of the more popular panic measures.

COLOURING YOUR HAIR

Rightly or not, society accepts without any qualms the right of women to disguise greying hair but rejects as risible the same behaviour in men. It's not fair, but that's the way it is – and don't think for a moment that people can't see the artfully applied hair dye, because they can.

THE COMB-OVER

Growing the hair at the side of the head long and then combing it over the bald patch is just about the worst thing you can do. Everybody laughs at a comb-over. So much so that it makes you wonder why people keep doing it.

SHAVING YOUR HEAD

At one time only two men in the world could get away with a shaved head, Mussolini and Yul Brynner. Now, however, shaving your head has become a fashion statement even for men who are not trying to conceal baldness. For those who use it as a way to disguise the ravages of age it has some advantages. It certainly gets rid of that moth-eaten look that baldies suffer from and it puts you in the same league as famous sportsmen and rock musicians. But before you take this step you need to be pretty sure that your head is the right shape and will look good when completely exposed. Not everyone can get away with this look, and on the wrong person it looks very silly indeed.

> Old age is the most unexpected of all the things that happen to a man.
>
> *Leon Trotsky*

THE PONY TAIL

Don't even go there. There is nothing, but *nothing*, that looks worse on an older man than a pony tail.

GROWING A BEARD

A beard as an antidote to baldness is not a great idea because it makes you look as though you've got your head on upside down. Some older men manage to look distinguished with a beard, but there are far more for whom it does nothing at all. The best tip is to ask the women in your life. Another thing older men really should avoid is designer stubble. On a 20- or 30-year-old it might look cool, but on you it looks as though you are too lazy to shave.

PUNCH GRAFTS

A punch graft is a type of cosmetic surgery where tufts of hair from the sides and back of the head are transplanted to the bald area. This is an expensive procedure and the results are by no means perfect. The grafts tend to grow in odd directions and give your hair that 'just crawled out of bed' look.

THE TOUPEE

A good-quality toupee is an expensive item. You can buy cheaper ones, but you might just as well stick a notice on your head that says 'I'm a bald guy in a toupee.' A good toupee, however, is not easily detectable. People may eventually catch on because hair that always looks perfect is a bit of a giveaway. If you never look as though you are urgently in need of a haircut, people will start to smell a rat, and as soon as they realise what you've been up to you will be the target for a good deal of cruel humour because there is something irresistibly funny about men who wear false hair.

CUT YOUR HAIR SHORT AND FORGET ABOUT IT

This is the only really sensible solution. Some people will make baldy jokes at your expense, but what the hell. At least you won't look like some desperate loser who is trying to hang on to the illusion of perpetual youth.

> How pleasant is the day when we give up striving to be young, or slender.
>
> *William James*

And the panic doesn't end there, for men tend to view later life as an affront to their manhood. They may be showing few signs of ageing yet still be feeling somehow diminished by the passing of the years. It doesn't seem long since they had to overcome the shock of being middle-aged, and now, having got quite comfortable with that idea, they are confronted with yet another change, only this time there is a lot more to worry about. To put the matter plainly, few of us can contemplate old age and eventual death with an air of calm acceptance. People react in different ways, but complete panic is quite common. Men who react in this way usually go into denial, and here are two of the better-known frantic attempts to regain a lost youth.

BUYING A FAST CAR

The connection between machismo and fast cars is too well known to require comment. But is this panic purchase going to help? In the short term it might. A man who relies on his car to project his personality (and many do) will feel energised by owning a powerful car. Other people, however, will snigger and write him off as yet another old man trying desperately to turn back the years. If you buy a convertible and race around with the top down while wearing a sporty-looking hat they will probably laugh at you openly – and, to be blunt, you have only yourself to blame.

SWAPPING THE WIFE FOR A NEWER MODEL

A much more serious male strategy is to divorce the wife in favour of a younger, more attractive partner. This is where the laughing stops. Whereas the fast car merely makes you look silly, a divorce causes real pain to all concerned. Because you entered into the relationship as a panic measure to try to stave off the ageing process there is a good chance that you and your new partner may not be well suited to each other. Your wife has had a lifetime to build up a relationship with you, and over the years you have learnt to adjust to each other's ways. It is doubtful whether you can establish a similarly close relationship with someone new, especially since you are obviously a thoroughly self-centred and insensitive person.

Women may also panic as they find themselves approaching later life, but they react differently from men. Their attitude to ageing relies heavily on three options.

COSMETICS

Society permits women certain strategies that are simply not available to their husbands. A woman is allowed, without fear of criticism, to colour her hair and use make-up to disguise her age. However, if you are going down this route, do choose a colour that looks natural. For an older woman to dye her hair black or auburn is just asking for trouble, and going for a frankly unnatural colour – the dreaded blue rinse, for example – looks even worse. If you go for something mousy you will be able to get away with it for years.

> The woman who tells her age is either too young to have anything to lose or too old to have anything to gain.
> *Chinese proverb*

CLOTHES

Women can also use clothing to create an impression of youthful-ness. As long they have a sense of style and good taste they will get away with making themselves look younger, and this will help them feel better about themselves. The danger lies in their taking this strategy too far: they may end up looking like 'mutton dressed as lamb'. Older women dressed in styles that are too young for them make themselves look silly and give everyone around them something to gossip about.

> So much has been said and sung of beautiful young girls.
> Why don't somebody wake up to the beauty of old women?
> *Harriet Beecher Stowe*

COSMETIC SURGERY

The other panic measure that is open to women is to have cos-metic surgery. You might object that men also opt for surgery, and it's true that this is a growing trend, but for the moment it is still largely a female preserve. For those who can afford it there is a whole catalogue of procedures that can restore a youthful look. Nips and tucks will do away with stretched skin; liposuction can remove unwanted fat; botox injections can erad-icate your wrinkles – and that barely scratches the surface of the many procedures that are available. Many women are made to feel better about themselves by means of surgery. On the other hand, the ageing process will always win in the end, and at some point it is necessary to give in gracefully. There are few things as scary as seeing an elderly woman with skin stretched taut by so many face lifts that she looks like a waxwork doll. An old face has about it a certain dignity of its own, and to destroy that with too many operations is not a sensible way to go about things. I remember at the Frankfurt Book Fair finding myself standing next to the widow of a famous American crooner who had just written her autobiography. Her face had been lifted so often that it had come to resemble a plastic mask. I'm sure that if she had let nature take its course she would have looked much better.

> The age of a woman doesn't mean a thing. The best tunes
> are played on the oldest fiddles.
>
> *Ralph Waldo Emerson*

THE VALUE OF ENTHUSIASM

I've mentioned it before, but it bears repetition: if I were allowed to name only one thing that is of benefit in later life, I would without the slightest hesitation pick enthusiasm. Look around and you will see that the people who live the most satisfying lives are those who have a positive and enthusiastic approach. This attitude of mind outweighs any number of other problems. You see plenty of people who are clearly overweight and who haven't taken any exercise in years who are nonetheless kept vibrant by their positive mental attitude.

> None are so old as those who have outlived enthusiasm.
>
> *Henry David Thoreau*

This is excellent news for those who are naturally of an enthusiastic disposition, but where does it leave everyone else? Most of us are a mixture of enthusiasm, habit and apathy. There are things we do just because we know we have to, and some things we try to put off doing altogether because we find them too boring or annoying to be bothered with. One of the problems of getting older is that it is easy to give up activities because they seem to take too much trouble.

Take, for example, people who have spent their whole lives cooking wonderful meals for the family. Once the children have left home, cooking is something a couple will do just for each other. Cooking for an audience of one is not as much fun as cooking for a group, but if they are lucky they will have enough visits from family and friends to keep their interest in cookery on the boil. But it is all too easy to tell yourself that cooking for two is just not worth the effort, that it's far quicker and easier to buy something ready-made from the supermarket. Then, in time, when one of the partners dies, the survivor is left with the prospect of cooking for one. This is when it is very easy to give cooking up altogether and simply graze on snacks and junk food.

Similarly, in later years you are likely to have some health problems, and it is quite easy to allow these to become an excuse for doing less. You can get caught up in a vicious circle: you do less so your apathy grows, and you respond by doing even less. Eventually your life can boil down to sitting around the house watching daytime TV. Can you imagine anything worse?

It is such a gradual seeping away of enthusiasm that is one of the main dangers for the elderly. It is therefore essential to have areas in your life about which you are enthusiastic. There must be something apart from mere habit that gets you out of bed every day and makes life worth living. And what you do is far less important than the way in which you do it. It is wonderful to have something in your life that really inspires you, but not everyone is that lucky. However, we can all apply enthusiasm to the things we do. Letting everyday things become a chore is only one short step away from giving them up altogether.

Thomas Alva Edison

If anyone doubts the effect enthusiasm can have on life they should read Edison's biography. Edison lived to the age of 84 and was granted his last patent the year before he died. His energy and self-confidence were phenomenal, his life was packed with the most extraordinary achievements, and he became known as 'the wizard of Menlo Park' and 'father of the electrical age'. We have Edison to thank for the electric light, the dictaphone, the mimeograph and the storage battery, not to mention a vast number of other devices. But not all of his work ended in success. Just like all inventors he had some ideas that either didn't work or were simply not commercial successes. But he never let that bother him one bit. On one occasion a young man sympathised with him that a particular series of experiments had not produced the expected result. Edison brushed aside the remark by pointing out that he now knew thousands of things that would not work and this was very valuable knowledge. He continued to work almost to the end of his life and never lost his curiosity or his flow of ideas.

To shore up enthusiasm you need to cultivate some new interests. It is important to get out of the house and spend time doing interesting things and meeting people. There are day centres where older people can go and join in activities with others of their age, but, to be honest, these always look deeply boring and you would have to be fairly desperate to join one. Do you really want to spend your time playing daft games or being taken on outings to 'places of interest' that might not be at all interesting?

> In his later years, Pablo Picasso was not allowed to roam an art gallery unattended, for he had previously been discovered in the act of trying to improve on one of his old masterpieces.
>
> *Anon.*

Just because you are older there is no reason at all why you should not be able to join in with the sort of activities enjoyed by the rest of society. If you are interesting, have a lively mind and are able to socialise with people of other generations, you will find that you are welcomed in all sorts of social circles. Older people who have time to spare can be a great asset to all sorts of clubs and societies (see 'The community' on page 76). Frequently, the younger members have limited leisure time and would be grateful for any help you could offer.

An old friend of mine called George retired and, having been a life-long bachelor, found himself with unlimited time to fill. Where we live there are numerous language schools catering for foreign students who come to learn English. George started offering coach tours to various places around the country, and they proved extremely popular. Not only did they provide a cheap way for the students to see a bit of the country, they also allowed whole groups of friends to go together. George was always on hand to sort out any difficulties, and because he was so much older than the students he was treated as a very popular father figure. Over time, his little business grew to be a great success. Had he wanted to he could easily have launched it as a proper commercial concern. But all he really wished for was something to keep his interest in life going. He certainly got that, and right up to the end of his life he continued to get cards and letters from former students who remembered him and his coach trips with great affection.

> The longer I live the more beautiful life becomes.
>
> *Frank Lloyd Wright*

To keep yourself interested, you need to set yourself goals. Decide what you are going to do and how long it should take you, and then work to achieve your goals. This takes some thought and self-discipline, but it is worth the effort because it will keep you active and interested. Even if you don't have any hobbies or interests you could try making a list of all the things that need doing around the house and then work your way through them. There is never any shortage of DIY jobs that need doing, and when you've finished with the house there is always the garden to think about. The aim should be to end each day with the feeling of a job well done, and to start the new day with plans for further work.

GRUMPY OLD MEN (AND WOMEN)

Just as an optimistic, positive outlook can improve your life, a negative outlook is very damaging. Some people as they grow older start to see nothing but faults in the modern world. This is very sad, but not uncommon. Some people seem to think that the world was only any good when they were young, and that it has been in decline ever since. They read newspapers whose content consists almost entirely of stories that can be summarised as 'Isn't it dreadful?' and 'Isn't it disgusting, it ought not to be allowed!'

Once you have developed a negative view it is only too easy to find things to feed it. All the bad things that are reported in the news simply provide more evidence that society is indeed going to the dogs. People who start down this road get a grisly kind of pleasure from bad news. They will constantly talk about disasters, serious illness and untimely death, moral lapses and political scandals. Eventually they can only talk to grumpy friends of their own age because everybody else either ignores or avoids them.

> If you carry your childhood with you, you never become older.
>
> *Tom Stoppard*

The best way to remain young is to be young at heart. You have to accept that the world has changed since your youth and realise that not all the changes are for the worse. Yes, we now face a threat from global terrorism, but on the other hand the former communist states are now free. Yes, AIDS is a terrible scourge, but think of all the advances medical science has made and all the diseases that can now be cured. No matter what is wrong with the modern world, you can point to some important improvements. There never was a Golden Age when all was right with the world, and there never will be. In every generation people do their best, and what they need from their elders is help and co-operation, not endless criticism.

WHERE TO LIVE?

Another crucial consideration when it comes to getting ready for retirement is your future living conditions. There are no right or wrong answers to the question 'Where to live?', but you do need to consider your options carefully. There is a strong temptation to opt for the status quo just because that is the easiest thing to do – but is it the wisest?

THE BIG MOVE

One of the favourite daydreams of middle-aged people is to retire to some idyllic spot to live out their days in surroundings that they find more congenial than those they have had to live in up to now. For all these years it has been necessary to live close to work, but now they have the freedom to choose some beautiful spot in the country, or even to move overseas and set up home in a favourite foreign country.

A big move like this has its advantages. First, you can move to a house where property prices are lower. This means that you could afford a bigger, more luxurious house, or, if you bought one of equivalent size to your former home, you would have some spare cash to play with. Second, because you are no longer working you would be able to move to pleasant rural areas where you could enjoy a tranquil existence free from hustle and bustle. If you opt to move abroad, then you might also find a warmer climate and an interesting local culture. These advantages are sufficiently seductive to lure many recently retired people abroad every year, but there's always a flip side. Here are some of the potential pitfalls to bear in mind:

- Separation from family, friends and familiar surroundings. When you first retire you may feel fighting fit and ready to take on a new challenge, but as you get older are you going to miss the comfort and familiarity of your old home? Will you be able to make new friends to take the place of those you've left behind? Will your family be able to come and visit you easily?

- If you decide to go abroad, will you find that the country where you may have spent happy holidays in the past is still as enjoyable when you live there all the time? A couple of weeks in the sun each summer is a very different thing from living in a sunny climate for months on end.
- How well would you fit in with the local community? They may be perfectly friendly when you are there as tourists, but would you be able to settle in and make friends with people whose whole way of life is quite different from what you are used to? Cultural differences often make it hard for people to get close to one another. If you want to be accepted in a new community you are the ones who have to change their ways, and you need to consider whether you could live life their way permanently.
- Do you speak the language? You might speak it well enough to get you through summer holidays, but will your language skills be up to the rigours of everyday life? Could you, for example, phone a local plumber and explain that your loo was blocked and the bathroom flooded? If you can't, then you have to ask yourself whether you would be willing to learn the language more thoroughly.
- How does the cost of living compare with that in the UK?
- Have you researched all legal and financial avenues? You need, for instance, to be sure that you will still be able to receive pension payments if you live overseas. Also, do you have to pay any local taxes? Are death duties punitive in the country in which you wish to live?

These are just some of the factors you should be considering if you're thinking about moving abroad. I've condensed them and others into a checklist:

Checklist 1

1. Do you have detailed knowledge of the place?
2. Do you speak the language, or would you be willing or able to learn?

3. Do you have local contacts? Would you be able to make friends with local people?
4. Do you have detailed knowledge of property prices and the cost of living?
5. Do you know what the place is like outside the tourist season?
6. Will you be able to tolerate the local climate?
7. Could you put up with separation from family and friends?
8. How do your family feel about you moving?
9. Would you be better off living abroad for just part of the year but keeping a base at home?
10. Have you considered the legal and financial situation?

Living abroad also raises problems over healthcare. Although you may receive excellent healthcare in many countries, you need to be quite sure that you can afford it. You need to be aware that recently the Department of Health has been considering withdrawing free NHS care for pensioners who live overseas for more than six months of the year. It hasn't happened yet, but it might be just a matter of time. Here's your medical checklist:

Checklist 2

1. If you are on medication, you need to take adequate supplies with you. It is quite possible that the exact medicines you use are not available overseas.
2. It is a good idea to take a reserve supply if possible. Running out of vital medicines is not something you would want to contemplate.
3. Keep a note of all the medicines you use in your wallet or handbag. If by any chance you get taken to hospital and are unconscious it will help the medical staff to understand the nature of your problems.
4. One of the first things you should do on arrival is to register with a local doctor. Unless you speak the language well you should try to find one who speaks English.
5. You should speak enough of the language to be able to describe obvious symptoms. If you can't say 'I have stomach ache' or 'I have a pain in my back', learn how to.
6. Remember that in the EU you're entitled to free or reduced-cost treatment, but you must register with the local health service.

There is, however, a less drastic alternative to moving abroad. Many older people make a habit of spending the winter months in a warmer climate and then return home for the summer. Thus they can avoid the worst of the British winter but still keep in close touch with family and friends at home. This can work well economically because they avoid paying out for expensive winter heating and lighting bills at home and they often save money by virtue of the lower cost of living abroad. This arrangement is often very popular with their family, too, because it gives them an excuse to take a winter holiday to visit their relatives abroad. In places where such winter visits are especially popular you often find a lively expatriate community.

STAYING IN YOUR OWN HOME

There are very strong reasons for people to want to stay in their own home. For a start you have worked hard to get the house just the way you like it. It is likely that you have all your friends and family nearby and would be reluctant to be parted from them. There are, however, a number of issues that arise from this decision.

First, any house needs constant attention. Over the years the fabric of the building wears out and bits have to be mended or replaced. The garden also has to be kept in good order. When you first retire you may well find that a bit of DIY and gardening is just what you need to keep yourself occupied and interested. But what about when you get older? Will you still have the energy, enthusiasm and strength to maintain your house? What if your partner dies – would you want to carry on in the house on your own, and if you did, would you be capable of doing so?

> Old age ain't no place for sissies.
>
> *H. L. Mencken*

Many people are quite determined to stay in their own home until their death. I know several people well into their eighties who are still quite happily living an independent life in the house they have occupied for the last fifty years. Then again, you may decide to stay in your house for, say, another ten years and then review the situation. Think about the options open to you and discuss them with your family now rather than be forced into a sudden move later on.

You can also, of course, remain in your own home even if you are unable to look after yourself. If you have regular visits from a health visitor, they may be able to organise extra help for you. Failing that, the local office of the Department of Health and Social Services will be able to offer advice. And if you are not entitled to help from the DHSS there are private companies that will provide help, though naturally you will need to pay for this yourself. One of these agencies is called Country Cousins, and it offers a range of services such as:

- meal preparation;
- light housework;
- shopping;
- home administration;
- personal laundry;
- companionship.

You can contact them at Country Cousins, 3rd Floor, West Point, Springfield Road, Horsham, West Sussex RH12 2PD (tel: 0845 601 4003; website: www.country-cousins.co.uk).

Checklist 3

1. Will your house suit you when you retire?
2. Once your children leave home, will the house be too big?
3. Will you be able to manage your house as you get older?
4. Do you need to get your hands on the equity tied up in your house? (See 'Cashing in on equity' on page 174.)
5. If you moved, what would you miss about your current home?
6. What would be the advantages of moving?
7. Are there any disadvantages?
8. You may want to postpone the decision, so at what age do you think you should reconsider?

SHELTERED ACCOMMODATION

Sheltered accommodation usually comprises a small development of flats or bungalows in which elderly people have their own separate accommodation but live in a community. There is a warden who looks after the residents and who is available to sort out problems. The advantage of this way of living is that you can retain your independence while having a safety net. Many people live very happy and contented lives in these communities safe in the knowledge that when things go wrong they are not alone. On the other hand, some older people feel that moving into sheltered accommodation is an admission that they are finally past it and ready for the scrapyard.

A FAMILY HOME

For many years it has been customary in Western societies – though less so in the more traditional areas of Mediterranean countries – that children leave their parents' home and set up house on their own. But this arrangement has slowly started to change.

First, there was the granny flat, or annexe. The children would set aside part of their accommodation for the use of one of their widowed parents (usually, but not always, the granny). On the plus side, Granny would often sell her own house and put some of the proceeds into helping the kids buy a house large enough for them all to live in. Also, Granny would be around to babysit and otherwise help out within the household. In return, Granny would have the security of having her family in close proximity if she needed help.

So far so good, but of course there are problems. For a start, the whole scheme depends on the enlarged family getting on well together, and that can never always be the case. Sometimes, having Granny interfering in family affairs causes tension and family rows. It is hard to live close to another adult and keep relations cordial.

> Age merely shows what children we remain.
>
> *Goethe*

Recently there has been a new development. Because house prices have rocketed, young people have found themselves unable to buy a home of their own. One solution has been for them to go into partnership with their parents and buy a home for the whole family. This is a much more radical scheme because it involves not just one widowed relative but a pair (possibly two pairs) of grandparents living with the family. Needless to say, for this to work a really good relationship between the members of the family is necessary. If people are pushed into such a scheme merely by economic forces, it is unlikely they will be able to cope with all the problems.

It is tempting to say that such a relationship simply wouldn't work, but, much to my surprise, I have met two families who live like this and would not have it any other way. It will be interesting to see whether this will be a major development in the future or whether it is just a passing fad or an option for the minority.

THE CARE HOME

The last option is to live in a care home. This is by far the least favoured solution, for few people relish the idea of being confined to a community of old people where they are looked after by strangers. Sadly, for some people it is the only answer. If you get to the stage where you are no longer able to look after yourself, you need constant attention, and you have no family members either willing or able to provide it, then a care home is probably where you'll live out your final years.

I've heard many elderly people say quite emphatically that they would rather be dead than go into a home, but despite some bad press there are many care homes that provide a high standard of care and comfort. To choose one you could look on the web at ukcare.net/, or try the nursing homes directory at www.ucarewe-care.com/.

THE UNCERTAINTY PRINCIPLE

Finally, it's again worth pointing out the obvious: the difficulty with planning for the future is that we never know how long we will live or what the state of our health will be. Any decisions we make are, at best, educated guesses influenced by our personal preferences. This leaves us with a tricky choice between staying put and hoping for the best or accepting that we need to move before that decision is forced upon us by circumstances. All of us hope that we retain enough of our faculties to enable us to live independently until we die, but that can't always be the outcome.

I know of one couple, now in their mid-seventies, who made plans some years ago to rent out their house and move into a flat near their relatives. They are the sort of people who pride themselves on being able to make sensible, rational decisions, and it seemed at the time the obvious thing to do. But when the time came to do it they found they were still in excellent health and enjoying their life very much. The husband still goes to his office each day and the wife has many interests that keep her occupied. They spend much of each year travelling all over the globe and they have no plans to cut down on their activities. Their date for moving into the flat was first postponed by four years and has recently been postponed again, this time indefinitely. It is easy to sympathise. Keeping to their accustomed lifestyle is probably a major factor in their continuing good health. To move would be to admit to themselves that they have, at last, reached old age, and it might well undermine their well-being.

> The tragedy of old age is not that one is old, but that one is young.
>
> *Oscar Wilde*

On the other hand, one of my elderly relatives flatly refused the option of sheltered accommodation until her condition deteriorated so much that she eventually ended up in a care home. Had she accepted the first option she would probably have been able to live independently for many more years. This is a classic example of what can happen if you don't make a move at the right time.

Making the wrong choice can make a major difference to the quality of your life in the future, so look hard before you leap, be decisive, and always remember that the world is your oyster.

FURTHER INFORMATION

* *Housing Options for Older People* by Louise Russell (Age Concern, ISBN 0862422876)

- *A Buyer's Guide to Retirement Housing* (Age Concern, ISBN 0862423392)
- *The* Which? *Guide to Buying Property Abroad* by Jeremy Davies (*Which?* Consumer Guides)
- *Retiring to Spain* by C. R. Holbrook (Age Concern, ISBN 0862423856)

LIFEPLAN QUESTIONNAIRE

To end this opening section of the book, which has dealt with the importance of starting afresh, here is a lifeplan questionnaire whose purpose is to give you the opportunity to focus your thoughts on how you want to spend your time in later years. As with the earlier questionnaire 'Who do you think you are, and who do you want to be?' (see page 24), there aren't any right or wrong answers because they depend entirely on your personal preferences, but some people find that working through a set of questions like this helps them to crystallise their thoughts. You may also find that these questions spark off others that are particularly relevant to your situation. Over a period of time your objectives change, so that whereas now you might find that your main objective is to spend time travelling, at a later date you might decide you'd like to be at home more so that you can enjoy your grandchildren as they grow up. The questionnaire relates not only to this section but to other parts of this book, so keep it handy, and in a few years' time you can try it again and see what changes you would like to make.

Section 1 – General

1. Are you looking forward to your later years?
2. Do you have fears about getting older?
3. If your children have not yet left home, how do you feel about the prospect?
4. Have you already started to make retirement plans or are you content to wait until later?
5. Do you see your later life as a new opportunity or does it worry you that the life you are used to is ending?
6. Are you looking forward to lots of new activities or would you rather just relax?

7. Have you talked with your partner about the things you'd like to do in retirement?
8. Do you like to plan for the future or do you let it take care of itself?

Section 2 – Work

1. How important is work to you?
2. What do you enjoy about your work?
3. What aspects of working do you dislike?
4. To what extent does your work define who you are?
5. Would retirement leave a hole in your life?
6. Do you like your work so much that you will continue until you drop?
7. Would you consider working part time?
8. If you worked part time, how many hours per week would you work?
9. Do you want to give up work at the first possible opportunity?
10. What things about your working life will you miss when you retire?
11. To what extent is your social life linked to your working life?
12. Would you like to start a new career?
13. Would you be keen to retrain for a new line of work?
14. Would you consider voluntary work of some sort?

Section 3 – Location

1. When you retire, do you want to continue living in the same place?
2. If you decided to move, where would you go?
3. Is making a break and starting somewhere new something that would excite and interest you?
4. Would you consider moving abroad?
5. Do you have friends and family you could join abroad?
6. Would you move in order to stay close to your children and grandchildren, or other members of your family?
7. Would you be prepared to leave family and friends here in order to live abroad?
8. Would you move to a smaller house in order to liberate some of the equity in your current home?

Section 4 – Leisure

1. Do you have hobbies and leisure interests to which you will devote more time when you retire?
2. If not, how do you intend to spend your time when you are retired?
3. Are there interests for which you've never had time that you would like to try now?
4. Will you enjoy a more leisurely pace of life?
5. If you're a man, do you intend to help your wife with more household chores when you're retired?
6. Will you enjoy having time for DIY and gardening, or will you pay people to do that sort of thing for you?

Two

Limitless Possibilities

When I was a young man and had just graduated from university it suddenly struck me that limitless possibilities lay before me. I could choose to do just about anything I wanted with my life. That was an intoxicating thought, but, of course, the feeling of freedom did not persist for long. Soon I had to make choices about a career and relationships, and eventually about a home and children. Within a few years, although my life was very comfortable, the possibilities were no longer limitless.

But as we get older we get a second go at making choices about life. The children are getting ready to fly the nest, the employment situation has changed, the mortgage is nearly or already paid off, and once again there is that feeling that almost anything we want to do is within our reach. But it's no good letting the rest of your life happen to you like a road accident. If you don't plan for it you will miss opportunities and end up feeling unfulfilled. It's time to think in a bit more detail about the things you would like to do.

WORK

You've only just finished work, so why would you want to go straight back? Well, for some people work is a rewarding experience they are loath to give up, and these days there are some very good reasons why older people should continue to work.

> Age to me means nothing. I can't get old – I'm working. I was old when I was 21 and out of work. As long as you're working, you stay young. When I'm in front of an audience, all that love and vitality sweeps over me and I forget my age.
>
> *George Burns*

MONEY

Once you retire and that salary is no longer paid into your bank account every month you will have to find a new way to live. It may be that you have a pension to fall back on, but even if you do it might not provide anything more than a fairly basic level of subsistence. Returning to work could be a way to bolster your earnings so that you can afford some of the luxuries of life as well as the necessities. Governments are constantly hinting that in future it might be necessary for people to work until the age of 70, so you could find that the decision is not even yours to take.

NEW STATUS

We hear a lot about ageism and the way in which employers discriminate against older workers. But that is only part of the story. Increasingly, employers are finding that older workers bring great advantages. They are often more experienced, better educated, politer and more conscientious than youngsters. Don't assume that just because you are retired an employer won't want you. You may find there is a pleasant surprise in store.

In the business world, and especially in the retail sector, diversity is the new buzzword. What it means is that businesses such as supermarkets that have to deal face to face with the public are at last discovering something that should have been obvious: they have found that people like to be served by 'real' people, i.e., people like themselves. For many years shop assistants in the UK have tended to be young, poorly educated (lacking not only formal education but also any real knowledge of the products they are selling), and seemingly devoid of basic social skills such as being polite and helpful to the customers. One way to tackle the problem is to hire people from outside this narrow group. The businesses concerned are not acting out of generosity or political correctness, but purely from self-interest. They have found that it makes good business sense to do this. That is a hopeful sign, because businesses only get really serious about an issue when there is money to be made from it.

One of the leaders in the field is the DIY chain B&Q. Not only have they made serious attempts to employ older staff, they have also started using them in their TV commercials. All the indications are that customers like this approach. They feel that the staff they are dealing with are more approachable and more likely to give them help and advice.

> Old age is not total misery. Experience helps.
>
> *Euripides*

Recently, I went into my local Tesco in search of a bottle of gin. I'm not a regular gin drinker so I spent a little time comparing brands and prices. Out of the corner of my eye I noticed that one of the shelf fillers, a man who looked to be in his seventies, was watching my progress. After a couple of minutes he came over to me and pointed out an own-brand gin with a plain white label. 'That's the one all the pensioners drink,' he told me. 'It's cheaper than all the others and just as good.' I decided to take his advice, and just as I was leaving with my bottle he called out, 'We do a good own-brand whisky as well if you're ever interested. I'm a Scot, so I know about whisky!'

That little bit of personal service was well worth the effort. I was pleased that someone had taken an interest in my purchase. After that he always remembered me and gave me a smile and a greeting whenever our paths crossed. It may not seem a hugely important marketing strategy, but it's probably worth more than any amount of advertising.

FULFILMENT

Do you like your work? Many people actually enjoy working. They find it gives them a sense of achievement and puts them in a social situation where they enjoy contact with their co-workers. Even if you didn't enjoy the job you retired from there might well be other work you could do that would make you happy. This is the time to sit down and think about what sort of work you might do.

Let's assume that you do want to work but don't, as yet, know what sort of work you might do. The first thing you're going to need is an up-to-date CV. It's quite likely that if you've been in the same job for years you haven't bothered to keep your CV in good repair, so you might well have to start from the beginning.

HOW TO WRITE A LETTER OF APPLICATION

People will go to great trouble to produce an impressive CV but regard the letter of application as of no real importance. Wrong, wrong, *wrong*! Research has shown that employers take more notice of the accompanying letter than of the CV. If you don't grab their attention from the first moment they might never even get as far as reading the CV.

Think of the letter of application as if you were being introduced to your new employer in person. What sort of impression would you want to make? You need to convey as much of this as possible in your letter. Why do you want the job? What marks you out from the crowd as being a particularly good applicant? Have you any experience or qualifications that set you apart from the other applicants? Make sure also that the letter is neat (preferably word-processed) and contains no grammatical mistakes or spelling errors. This should seem obvious, but I have received plenty of letters from people whose lack of language skills has ruled them out right at the start.

Norman Wisdom
Now in his eighties, Norman Wisdom has been entertaining the public since before most of us were born. He typically played the well-intentioned but accident-prone little guy who, though often knocked down (often literally), never fails to get up again and carry on. In his tight-fitting jacket and battered cloth cap he blundered through life from one misfortune to another. The humour wasn't subtle, but it has always been popular. There has never been a time when he has been forgotten by his fans, and for him retirement was never an option. Because his brand of comedy is readily understood even by those who speak no English, his international following is huge, and in recent years he made headlines when he visited Albania. He still tours and records, and is talking of making another film. In 1995 he was awarded the OBE, and in the New Year's Honours List of 2000 he gained a knighthood. His only problem is that, unless restrained, he still tries to tumble about.

HOW TO WRITE YOUR CV

If your CV is merely a recital of qualifications gained and jobs you have done, it won't attract much attention. Employers are looking for that one person who has something special to offer. Their attention span is quite limited, and if you appear to be just another run-of-the-mill applicant you are unlikely to get to the interview stage. A good CV is a selling document that will persuade prospective employers that you are exactly the person they have been looking for. Before you even start you should spend some time considering the following areas:

- Think about skills you have that someone might find useful. Do you speak any languages? Do you drive (and have a clean driving licence)? Do you have computer skills? Are you good with people? You may find that you have skills that, though they went unused in your last job, could make you just the person a new employer is looking for. Always try to include one item that makes you stand out from the crowd; it can be anything that will pique the reader's curiosity. Have you hiked the Appalachian Trail? Do you keep poisonous snakes? Have you studied Chinese? It doesn't matter too much what your claim to fame is as long as it's quirky enough to make the employer want to know more about you.

- You need to assess your character as honestly as possible. This can be a tough one, but it is important to get it right. Remember that employers have read hundreds of these things before and are a bit jaded at the prospect of yet another keen, hard-working, honest, reliable employee with a bubbly personality and excellent interpersonal skills. Put yourself in the employer's place and try to think of the qualities you have that would make you want to employ yourself. Make sure that you present your age as an advantage. Be prepared to argue your corner on this one. Some employers need a bit of convincing that older workers are better. With the right arguments, they can be persuaded to take a chance on you.
- Think about the nature of the employer's business, and try to find reasons why you would be an asset. Do you have relevant experience? Are you full of good ideas for developing the business further? As an older person it is likely that you have plenty of contact who might prove useful. Make sure that the employer knows that your age and experience would work strongly in the company's interests.

When you've decided on the text, make sure that you present the CV properly. This means typing it clearly and in an orderly fashion on one side of an A4 sheet. *Never* send in anything handwritten. Use a computer, and if you aren't computer literate pay someone to do it for you. Keep it plain and clear. Don't be tempted to use 'interesting' typefaces or strange design flourishes as these will only irritate people.

Finally, a word of warning: don't claim qualifications or experience you don't actually have. This counts as fraud, and employers are getting wise to it. Anything about yourself you commit to paper must bear up to close scrutiny.

Find an aim in life before you run out of ammunition.
Arnold Glasow

THE INTERVIEW

Some people dread interviews, but if handled properly they are an excellent opportunity for you to convince a prospective employer that you are right for the job. If you want to succeed in an interview, however, there are a few things you need to remember.

APPEARANCE

Think carefully about what sort of business you are applying to. It's no good turning up in your best interviews, weddings and funerals suit if the job you're applying for is in a place where everyone wears jeans and T-shirts. You want to create the feeling that you would easily blend in and quickly become part of the team.

PUNCTUALITY

Do get there on time. There are few things more irritating than someone who's late. On the other hand, don't arrive so early that it looks as if you have nothing better to do with your time.

MANNER

One of the advantages of being older is that you have more confidence. The days when people made you nervous are long gone. You should aim to appear relaxed and quietly confident – but not so confident that you seem cocky. Give a firm (but not bone-crushing) handshake, make eye contact, and smile pleasantly. Answer questions with enough detail to be convincing, but resist the urge to ramble. Try to strike up a rapport with the interviewer. This is especially important if the interviewer is the boss you will be working for. Try to get him or her to reveal information about him/herself. It is amazing how little things can create a bond. During an interview I once went to it turned out that the boss had lived just round the corner from me when we were kids in Edinburgh, and we'd gone to the same school. This may not have been the reason he offered me the job, but it certainly did me no harm.

ATMOSPHERE

Take note of how the interviewer and any other members of staff you meet behave. Are they friendly and welcoming? Do the staff seem happy, and do they seem at ease with the boss? This is your opportunity to delve into the company and find out whether you want to work there. Ask plenty of questions, not only because it will make you seem keen but because the answers will reveal what sort of person you are dealing with. Always trust your instincts. If you feel in any way uneasy about the boss or the company don't try to talk yourself out of it and force yourself to take the job because it is the 'sensible' thing to do. If you feel uneasy, it is for a reason. You have been picking up non-verbal signals that tell you quite clearly that all is not well and that you are not going to be happy in this job, so let it pass and look for another.

THE SHORTLIST

It is normal, especially if there have been a lot of applicants, to pick out the best, put them on a shortlist and re-interview. If you get invited to a second interview that's a very encouraging sign, but you still have a lot to do before the job is yours. Put your thinking cap on and imagine that the job is yours already – what would you do? You need to be able to show that you have valuable ideas right from the start. Companies don't like to spend time and money on training new people. If you can show that you would be an asset from the start then you will be streets ahead.

BEING THE OLDEST PERSON IN THE OFFICE

Your application is successful, but now you might find that you are the oldest person in the office. How will you handle the situation? Will you mind taking orders from people many years your junior? Much will depend on your attitude. If you disapprove loudly of the way the youngsters dress, speak and behave, you aren't going to make many friends. Any critical thoughts you may have about the younger generation should be kept strictly to yourself.

> The great thing about getting older is that you don't lose all the other ages you've been.
>
> *Madeleine L'Engle*

The questions in the following chart will help you establish the strength of your various motivations. Start at the top of the left-hand column and move downwards answering the questions as you go. Give yourself three points for each 'yes' answer. Move to the next column to the right as soon as you encounter a 'no' answer, or if you get to the bottom of a column without ever having answered 'no'. At the end add up your scores from each column and you will see which are your strongest motivations

Money	Control	Fulfilment	Activity
Do you expect to be financially comfortable when you retire?	Do you enjoy the feeling of being in charge of things?	Did/does your work give you a sense of fulfilment?	Are you a person who needs to keep busy?
↓	↓	↓	↓
Will you need to work part time to pay for extras?	Is being in control important to your self-image?	Would retirement destroy that feeling?	Would retirement involve a loss of activity?
↓	↓	↓	↓
Will you have to work part time just to make ends meet?	Would you experience a loss of control when you retired?	Would lack of fulfilment affect your self-image?	Would being less active affect your self-image?
↓	↓	↓	↓
Will you be able to get a job that pays enough to maintain your lifestyle	Would being less in control worry you?	Would you find it hard to adjust to a life that lacked fulfilment through work?	Would you be uncomfortable with a life that is less busy than the one you lead now?
↓	↓	↓	↓
Is your future income a major source of anxiety?	Do you worry that you might not be able to replace the feelings of control you enjoyed before retirement?	Would you be able to find other ways to experience fulfilment once you retired?	Do you fear that you might suffer a loss of activity when you retire?

If you find that impossible, then you are in the wrong job. If you take the trouble to be helpful and approachable you will soon find that people many years younger than you are quite willing to ask you for advice. Most of them will be happy to treat you like a Dutch uncle, as long as you make an effort to get on with them. If you learn to show interest in subjects that are important to them they will be very happy to explain things to you. If handled properly, there can be a mutually useful flow of ideas and information.

FURTHER INFORMATION

- *The Complete Idiot's Guide to Getting the Job You Want* by Marc Dario (Alpha Books, ISBN 0028627237).
- *Getting Interviews* by Kate Wendleton (Career Press, ISBN 1564144488).
- *Interviews and Assessments: The Insider Guide to Succeeding at Selection and Getting the Job You Want* by Brian Sutton (Spiro Press, ISBN 1858358205).
- *The Secrets to Getting a Job* by Philip Garside (Hyland House Publishing, ISBN 1864470135).
- Also, the Third Age Employment Network (TAEN) is a network of member organisations whose shared objective is to ensure better opportunities for mature people to work, earn and learn, thus meeting the needs of employers and the economy. TAEN is a leading campaigner on all matters related to age and employment, and you can find them on the web at www.taen.org.uk.

TRAINING AND EDUCATION

You might find that having spent many years in one type of work you have missed out on some key skills. For example, it is not at all uncommon for older people to lack computer skills. Why not take the time to retrain and gain skills that will make you more employable? Alternatively, you might fancy learning for pleasure. Is there a subject that has always interested you that you have never had time to pursue? This could be your opportunity, and there are several ways to make the most of it.

> Education is the best provision for old age.
>
> *Aristotle*

GOING SOLO

The very cheapest option is to pick a new skill that you want to acquire, find a good book on the subject and set out to master it on your own. Some people thrive on self-teaching of this sort.

EVENING CLASSES

If book-learning sounds a little too solitary, you could always sign up for a proper course of instruction. There are dozens of courses available in all sorts of locations. If it's a long time since you had any formal teaching and you are not sure how good a student you will be, then why not start with something simple like an evening class? These are usually organised locally and often make use of schools that would otherwise be empty at that time of day. Evening classes are normally quite cheap, but even so, the instruction offered is of a good quality and frequently leads to exams that will provide you with new qualifications. It is particularly easy to pick up computer skills in this way as these courses are the most popular and seem to be offered just about every-where. An evening class is also a great place to acquire or brush up language skills.

The variety of courses offered by evening classes leaves you spoilt for choice. You can learn anything from flower-arranging to yoga, from carpentry to pottery. Some of the courses are purely for amusement, but quite a few will offer some sort of qualification at the end. The advantage of such courses is that they don't cost much and are held in your local area so you don't have to make a long journey in the dark to get there – for the best time to start a new course is in the autumn when, as the nights start to draw in, people fancy having something to do during the long evenings.

Finding such courses is easy. Libraries usually have lists of those that are available in their area. Quite often they also have a notice-board on which people who run courses are allowed to advertise. Also, in the autumn many libraries hold a fair at which all sorts of local bodies, including those offering evening classes, are allowed to run a stall and try to recruit new members. Your local newspaper is another good source of information: it will often publish details of courses and the people who run them. Many local colleges have a mailing list, and it is useful to get your name added to it so that you are automatically informed of new developments.

> I grow old learning something new every day.
>
> *Solon*

DISTANCE LEARNING

If you want to take training and/or education more seriously, you need to go to the next level. There are plenty of private colleges that offer distance learning courses, so you need to choose carefully because the quality of the tuition varies drastically. Try to pick a course that has a national reputation, and if possible join one that has been recommended by someone whose judgement you trust. This sort of learning can be quite expensive so you want to make sure that it will give you value for money. Courses of this sort usually provide you with a personal tutor who will look at your work and send back comments. This gives you the advantage of working at home but still having some human contact.

If that sounds like the sort of teaching you want, then here are a couple of places you should consider:

- ICS (International Correspondence Schools), the one that springs to everyone's mind. Visit www.icslearn.co.uk, where you can request a course guide. Alternatively, to speak to a course adviser and discuss your goals, freephone 0800 056 3983, or email icscourseadvisors@ics-uk.co.uk. Enquire about their easy payment plans.
- The National Extension College, a charity set up to provide learning opportunities for people of all ages. They do a wide range of courses in a huge variety of subjects. You can contact them by phone (01223 400200), fax (01223 400399), email (info@nec.ac.uk) or via their website (www.nec.ac.uk).

Tina Turner

For sheer vitality, Tina Turner is a hard act to beat. Anyone who has seen her stage show can testify that she puts into it every ounce of energy she has. Her ability to defy age is legendary; even when she was over 50 it was hard to believe that this sexy woman with a powerful voice was not at least ten years younger. There are plenty of things women can do to look good despite their age, but the one thing that can never be faked is vitality, and Turner, now over 60, still has this by the ton.

TAKING A DEGREE

If you really want to study a subject thoroughly and get a degree, why not go back to college? Most universities are very keen to encourage older students, and even if you never gained any formal qualifications in your youth you may find that a college will still admit you. In fact, there are some colleges that specialise in taking mature students. If you happen to live in the UK you could try London's Birkbeck College or, of course, the Open University, both of which are ideal suited to helping older students and who include distance learning in the range of services they offer.

- To contact Birkbeck College, phone 0845 601 0174, email admissions@bbk.ac.uk, or visit their website at www.bbk.ac.uk.

- You can find the Open University by email (General-Enquiries@open.ac.uk) or by phone (01908 858585). Their website is at www.open.ac.uk.

Colleges of further education are also especially useful because they offer a great variety of full- and part-time courses, anything from hairdressing to computer repair. You will find them listed in the *Yellow Pages*.

Any kind of college degree that's worth having will be both time-consuming and expensive. At the Open University, for example, courses are taken in modules and vary in price. Generally, a 60-point module costs between £400 and £700, and for an honours degree you will need to get a minimum of 360 points. Most modules are worth 30 or 60 points. Fee waivers, student loans and hardship funds are available, and the average time taken to complete a degree is six years. On the other hand, a degree will make you much more valuable to potential employers. Before you start, you must convince yourself that you really have the stamina to see the thing through to the end. Can you afford to invest so much time in study? A degree course is really a *lot* of work, so before you sign up you need to be sure you can make the commitment in terms of time and energy.

Another thing you need to think through is how you will cope in a place that is populated mainly by young people. All day every day you will be surrounded by people young enough to be your children. Some people find the energy and enthusiasm of youngsters very stimulating; others just find the kids immature, noisy and irritating. You have to ask yourself whether you could cope. When you apply to a college you will probably be invited for an interview, so when you go there, spend some time wandering around and soaking up the atmosphere. It might be fun to visit a college campus, but could you stand it all the time? Bear in mind that even if you like young people, they might well be wary of you. Making friends with people who are 30 or more years your junior could be difficult. You need to decide whether you would be able to cope if you didn't make any friends.

> And in the end, it's not the years in your life that count. It's the life in your years.
>
> *Abraham Lincoln*

UNIVERSITY OF THE THIRD AGE

For UK readers, it is worth mentioning the University of the Third Age (usually known as U3A), an excellent organisation that runs cheap courses in a wide variety of subjects aimed exclusively at older learners. It is not just a good place to learn but also an excellent way to make new friends. If this appeals to you, the national office is at 19 East Street, Bromley, Kent BR1 1QH (tel: 020 8466 6139; fax: 020 8466 5749). The website can be found at www.u3a.org.uk.

DfES

Finally, there is a special section for adult learners on the website of the Department for Education and Skills. You can find it by going to www.dfes.gov.uk.

THE COMMUNITY

If training and education don't appeal to you now that you're retired or working much less than you used to, why not devote some of your time and energy to helping the community? People sometimes feel that only work that is done in return for money counts as 'real' work; they see voluntary work as second best, a poor substitute for the real thing. This attitude is misguided, because without an army of volunteers many very important organisations would simply not survive. It also overlooks a strange quirk of the human psyche which is that people will happily work with far more energy and enthusiasm when they are volunteers than when they are being paid. There is something about payment that turns any activity into a chore. It is quite irrational, but then much of the time people are irrational.

> One of the signs of passing youth is the birth of a sense of fellowship with other human beings as we take our place among them.
>
> *Virginia Woolf*

WHAT COULD YOU DO?

Do you have any special skills that you could offer? There are some fairly obvious skills that are much in demand. For example, people who are computer literate are always useful, as are people who understand financial matters, or who can speak a second language. But if you don't have skills of that sort you may well have others that don't seem very special to you but which are of great use to others. If you can cook, if you know how to fix broken-down cars, if you can put up a set of shelves – all these are skills that might come in handy in the voluntary sector. Even if you have a flair for arranging flowers you might find yourself in demand at the local church. The possibilities are limitless. Try answering the following questions to get some idea of the direction you should take:

1. How many hours per week would you be prepared to dedicate to voluntary work?
2. Have you any professional qualifications that might be useful to the community?
3. Have you any skills that would be of use?
4. Do you prefer to work in an office/home environment, or do you enjoy working outdoors?
5. Are you good with people?
6. Do you enjoy looking after people who are in some way disabled?
7. Is it important to you to be surrounded by other people, or do you prefer to work alone?
8. Are you good with youngsters, or do you prefer people who are nearer to your own age?
9. Have you the persistence to work hard even though you aren't getting paid?
10. Is there anything you really hate doing?
11. Would you rather help people in your own community?
12. Would you enjoy charity work in aid of people overseas?
13. Are there issues of religion, ethnicity or political affiliation that would influence where you choose to work?
14. Are you well aware of opportunities in your neighbourhood, or do you need to do a bit of research to find out what is available?

HOW DO I GET STARTED?

Now that you have some idea of what you're looking for, we can discuss ways in which you might offer your help.

LOCAL COUNCILS

The obvious place to start is in your local area. In all small communities there is usually a governing body such as a parish council. These bodies always need volunteers, and because working people often find it hard to give their valuable time, much of the burden is carried by retired people. These local bodies might not be hugely powerful or influential, but they do concern themselves with issues that are very important to the local community, so they are not to be despised. Often local issues have a more direct influence on people's lives than the big issues tackled by politicians.

SCHOOLS

Local schools are also a good place to offer your help. Many schools employ learning support assistants (LSAs) to give one-to-one help to youngsters who have learning difficulties. You don't need to be a qualified teacher to do this work, you just need to like kids and have a lot of patience. Working with youngsters is particularly rewarding because you get to see the difference you make to their performance. There is a special satisfaction in helping someone to overcome difficulties and succeed in areas where they are accustomed to failure.

Another valuable service older people can provide for schools is to become a lollipop person. It takes up only a small part of your day, and younger children especially tend to treat lollipop people as personal friends to whom they can chat. If you like kids, then this is a pleasant and valuable job that everyone appreciates.

Remember, all work involving contact with children requires a police check. The process is quite straightforward: you simply fill in a short form giving all your personal details, and assuming there is nothing on your record to indicate that you might be a danger to children the school will be given the all clear and you will be allowed to start work.

If you don't feel that you can work with kids directly, don't let that put you off. Schools need help in all sorts of other ways, and they are always short of cash. If you have any special talent that might be of use you can be pretty sure you will be needed. Can you cook? One of the jobs regularly on offer is that of school dinnerlady. If you have experience in business you might be very effective working as a member of the board of governors. If you are good at making money you could lend a hand with fundraising. You will find that you only have to approach a school looking even marginally useful and you will be seized and pressed into service in some way.

Moreover, if you enjoy working with children, there are all sorts of openings outside the school environment, from birth onwards. Why not apply to help out at a local mother and toddler group, or you might consider working with cubs, brownies, scouts and guides. You can contact them at The Scout Association, Gilwell Park, Chingford, London E4 7QW (information centre tel: 0845 300 1818, local call rate); or Girlguiding UK (tel: 0800 169 5901).

> How does one keep from growing old inside? Surely only in community. The only way to make friends with time is to stay friends with people . . . Taking community seriously not only gives us the companionship we need, it also relieves us of the notion that we are indispensable.
>
> *Robert Macafee Brown*

WRVS

Looking beyond your immediate locality, there are many other ways of helping out. One lady I know quite well does a meals-on-wheels round for pensioners in her area. She refers to them as 'my old ladies' even though at 83 she is older than many of her clients. She also delivers the parish magazine and does a weekly shopping run for people who can't get about on their own.

If this sort of charity work is what you want then an excellent place to enquire is the WRVS (the Women's Royal Voluntary Service, though men are now allowed to join so they simply call themselves the WRVS). If you have ever been in hospital you will almost certainly have seen the WRVS lady come round with her trolley and offer you a book, but this is only a tiny part of what they do. Their website (www.wrvs.org.uk) describes their work as follows: 'WRVS provides a range of services to help people in need who might otherwise feel lonely and isolated. We work with other charities and organisations, local authorities and the NHS, meeting needs in communities throughout England, Scotland and Wales. Volunteers play a vital role in everything we do: over 95,000 of them – both men and women – give up their time to help other people and to make life better in their communities. Together with WRVS employees they deliver professional services with a personal touch.'

> Sure I'm for helping the elderly. I'm going to be old myself some day.
>
> *Lillian Carter (when in her eighties)*

You can contact them at WRVS, Garden House, Milton Hill, Steventon, Abingdon, Oxfordshire OX13 6AD (tel: 01235 442900; fax: 01235 861166; email: enquiries@wrvs.org.uk).

FUNDRAISING

Charities are always on the lookout for volunteers and they provide a huge variety of opportunities. The most basic charity job is rattling a collecting tin on a Saturday morning at your local shopping centre. This might not be a fun-filled way to spend your weekend, but it is the way in which charities survive, and without someone to do this tedious work many of them would perish. You will find appeals for volunteers:

- on church noticeboards;
- on parish or town council noticeboards;
- in parish magazines;
- in libraries;
- advertised on local shop windows.

CHARITY SHOPS

Many charities run their own shops which are staffed by volunteers. If you like meeting people then working in a charity shop might be just the thing for you. Shop work can be physically quite demanding and you may spend a large part of the day on your feet, so you need to be in good health to consider this option.

Mother Teresa
'By blood, I am Albanian. By citizenship, an Indian. By faith, I am a Catholic nun. As to my calling, I belong to the world. As to my heart, I belong entirely to the Heart of Jesus.' This diminutive Albanian nun became world famous for her work among the destitute and dying of Calcutta. It was not just her personal qualities of love and compassion that impressed people, it also became clear that she was a

formidable organiser, and in spite of her religious calling she was in no way naive or incapable of making tough decisions. It is inevitable that someone with so much influence would have her critics, and Mother Teresa was not universally admired, but no one has ever denied the enormous zest she brought to her tasks. Eventually her organisation had almost 4,000 members and had established 610 foundations in 123 countries. Almost to the end of her days she remained in personal charge of the work to which she devoted her life.

WORKING WITH PEOPLE

If you really like working with people you might consider a job that puts you in close contact with members of the public. Do you have what it takes to work in a shelter for the homeless, for example? Would you be happy to take hot soup to those living rough on the streets? There are also opportunities to visit people in hospital or to befriend those serving time in prison. These jobs can be emotionally demanding and not everyone is suited to them, but if you could do it, you would be making a contribution to the lives of people who need your help.

COUNSELLING

Similarly, counselling can be of immense benefit to those on the receiving end. In recent years, giving people advice and listening to their problems has become a major activity, and much of it is carried out by volunteers. Maybe the best example is that of the Samaritans, who run their famous telephone line for those who are desperate and suicidal.

But not everyone can be a Samaritan. Those who apply undergo a rigorous selection procedure and are put through a very demanding training course before they are accepted. The work is tough, and the emotional toll can be high. A friend who has been a Samaritan for many years told me that, just like a doctor, you have to get used to the fact that you can't help everybody. In some cases you will fail, and the person you were trying to help will end up committing suicide. Could you handle that? If you are strong enough to bear such strain, then the satisfaction you will get from being able to help some of your clients is enormous. You can contact the Samaritans at Upper Mill, Kingston Road, Ewell, Surrey KT17 2AF (tel: 08457 909090 (UK, local call rate), 1850 609090 (Republic of Ireland, local call rate); email: international@samaritans.org).

There are many other charities who will use people who already have a qualification in counselling. So if this is the sort of work you would like to do then you should look around for the appropriate course and get yourself trained. The place to start is the British Association for Counselling and Psychotherapy, BACP House, 35–37 Albert Street, Rugby, Warwickshire CV21 2SG (tel: 0870 443 5252; fax: 0870 443 5161; email: bacp@bacp.co.uk; website: www.bacp.co.uk).

I run a helpline for the parents of gifted children and can vouch for the satisfaction you feel when you help people. Because giftedness is not well understood by most people, and because the public and education system used to have a very negative view of gifted children, it was quite common for mothers to phone up in a highly emotional state. Being able to offer help and reassurance was a good feeling.

> Growing old is no more than a bad habit that a busy person has no time for.
>
> *André Maurois*

OTHER OPTIONS

There is only room here to touch on a few of the possibilities that are available, for there are many charities that need voluntary help – big ones such as Oxfam, the NSPCC and the RSPB, but also many others you have probably never heard of. If you want to do some charity work but don't know where to start, you can go to Charity Choice (their website is at www.charitychoice.co.uk), which provides an encyclopaedia of charities from which you can choose. You can buy a copy of the encyclopaedia but it is very expensive, so you might want to see if your local library has a copy in its reference section.

The main thing to remember is that whoever you are there is an important contribution you can make for the benefit of other people. It is no exaggeration to say that some people manage to do more good in the world after they retire than they ever do during their working lives. So have a go, and surprise yourself with just how much you can achieve.

TRAVEL

At one time, retirement was all about settling down and pursuing a quiet life at home. Now almost everybody looks forward to retirement because it will give them the leisure to travel more. At last they are no longer forced by the tyranny of school holidays to go at the peak of the season. Also, they no longer have to restrict themselves to a meagre fortnight's summer holiday. With no work to get back to they can go further and stay away for longer.

Almost all the couples I have come across who are on the brink of retirement seem to be planning some sort of marathon trip as a reward for all their years of hard labour. No longer is a couple of weeks in the Med regarded as an exciting adventure; people now are looking further afield for their adventures. Australia and New Zealand are obvious destinations, and the USA is a magnet for many. There are also many older people who want to visit really far-flung places in search of adventure.

> In old age one should do something monumental.
>
> *Xiao Qian*

A development that is of particular interest to older people is the DIY holiday. This has been made possible by the advent of low-cost airlines and the internet. You no longer have to have the type of holiday you take dictated to you by the travel companies. If you are willing to book early, or if you don't mind snapping up what is available at short notice, you can get very cheap tickets to a wide variety of destinations. The following low-cost airlines offer a 'no frills' service, but the financial saving is well worth a small amount of inconvenience:

- Ryanair
  Their website is www.ryanair.com, or you can phone 0871 246 0000. Office hours are from 09.00 to 17.45 on weekdays and

Saturdays, and 10.00 to 17.45 on Sundays. My experience of Ryanair has so far been entirely positive. Flights have been punctual, the service is good and, most important of all, the fares are really low.

- Easyjet
  easyJet Airline Company Limited, easyLand, London Luton Airport, Bedfordshire LU2 9LS (tel: 0871 7 500 100; website: www.easyjet.com).

I can't say that I have ever regretted travelling in this way. All the flights I have taken have been efficiently run and surprisingly punctual – and most important of all, the fares are low. The only disadvantage I have found is that foreign airports used by the low-cost companies can be very small places stuck out in the middle of nowhere. For example, you need a twisted sense of humour to suggest that Frankfurt-Haan has even the remotest geographical connection with the city of Frankfurt. However, there are always coach services provided to bring you back to civilisation; alternatively, you can hire a car and make your own way to your destination.

USING THE INTERNET

Going online to find a holiday requires some persistence, but it is well worth the effort. On the face of it this may seem a rather insecure way to make your plans. When they hear of this way of booking holidays for the first time most people are filled with suspicion and doubt. What if the whole thing is a scam and the 'owner' turns out to be a crook who takes your money and runs? What if the pictures on the website are only for show and the real accommodation turns out to be substandard? What if the whole place is much less interesting than it seems from the pictures on the website? All these questions and more run through your head when you book online.

HOTELS

If you want to stay in a hotel, your task is quite easy. Most tourist resorts have a website that lists all the hotels, gives details of location and room prices, and grades them according to some sort of star system. You can usually see photographs of the hotels as well. All you have to do is read through the details until you find one that suits your needs. You can make your booking online and you will normally get an email confirmation showing the dates you have booked and a record of the deposit you have paid. Tourist offices are obviously concerned that the customers get a good deal and will do their best to make sure that the accommodation you see advertised is exactly what you get.

SELF-CATERING

If you want a self-catering holiday you can still book online but the process is a little more complicated. As with the hotels, most self-catering apartments and houses are advertised on sites run by the appropriate local tourist authority. Rather than go through an agency, you get in touch with the owners of the property you want to rent and make your booking directly with them.

My experience is that on the whole the advantages of this type of holiday outweigh the disadvantages. The main advantage is that you are booking directly with the owner and you are not paying fees to any middlemen. This can make a big difference to the price. Most of the owners I have dealt with have been completely honest and were concerned to provide a good, efficient service; they are, after all, keen to avoid any complaints because no one wants their property to be struck off the list of recommended holiday homes.

I have been booking holidays in this way for some years and have had a few problems but never a complete disaster. In northern Spain we did once find ourselves sharing the accommodation with a large family of mice, but, to be fair, it was a large, rambling farmhouse and small rodents were to be expected. On another occasion we stayed in Thonon on the shores of Lake Geneva. The information provided by the local tourist office suggested that this was a lively, happening kind of place where there was never a dull minute thanks to the wonderful summer festival that took place each year. This turned out to be a great exaggeration. The town was very pleasant by day and had splendid facilities for swimming. By night, however, the place died. There *was* a summer festival, but it was a rather low-key affair that lacked much in the way of excitement.

> To me, old age is always fifteen years older than I am.
> *Bernard Baruch*

Quite often you come across properties owned by British families who take their own holidays there and then rent the place out for the rest of the year. This makes the whole arrangement much more convenient. You can phone the owner and have a chat about the property and also get the inside story on the locality. All the British owners I have come across have been enormously enthusiastic about both their property and the area in which it is situated. One man spent about 45 minutes giving me huge amounts of useful information and advice. He was clearly in love with the area and could not stop singing its praises. When we got there we found he had spoken nothing but the truth, and we had such a splendid time that we went back to the same place the following year, thus breaking a family rule that we should never repeat a holiday.

Good sources for ideas about hotels and properties, and information on all aspects of travel, include:

- The *Sunday Times*
  This is indispensable for anyone looking for a holiday. The articles are often interesting and entertaining, but the thing most people buy it for is the small ads which offer a huge variety of places to stay and ways of getting there.

- The *Independent*
  The Saturday edition has a travel supplement which contains interesting articles. Recently there have been guides showing the best way to spend 48 hours in various cities. The one for Cambridge (where I live) was entirely accurate, and the one for Ljubljana, which we took with us on holiday, was very useful.

- *Condé Nast Traveller*
  This is an excellent magazine for anyone who loves to travel. It is packed with useful information. You can buy it from your newsagent, and there is also a website at
  www.cndtraveller.com

PREPARATION

Preparing for a holiday before you go seems such an elementary precaution that it should hardly need to be mentioned. Alas, that is far from being so. A lot of people are quite happy to set off for some place they have never heard of without a thought for what it's like or even, except in very general terms, where it is. Just recently a friend was telling us with great enthusiasm about a forthcoming holiday in the south of France. When we asked where exactly she was going she told us that it was Brittany. Nothing would persuade her that Brittany is in fact in the north-west of the country. We had to get out a map and show her.

> A man is not old as long as he is seeking something.
>
> *Jean Rostand*

THE IMPORTANCE OF RESEARCH

A bit of local knowledge goes a very long way to making sure that you are not disappointed in your holiday. First, you need to know *exactly* where you are going. If it's a resort, you should find out what sort of resort it is. They are definitely not all the same. If you are in the 50-plus age group you are unlikely to feel at home in a place that is overrun by youngsters who have come abroad for two weeks of sun, sea and sex (not to mention lashings of booze and some very loud music). Even resorts right next to each other can be very different. For example, in north-east Spain you will find the charming town of L'Escala. It has almost no British tourists but thousands of French ones. Just along the coast is Estartit, which is full of the sort of Brits who favour shaved heads, tattoos and multiple body-piercings. It will obviously make a big difference to your holiday which of these places you choose. Get the wrong one and you will wish you'd stayed at home.

You also need to know as much as you can about the surrounding area. Are you a culture vulture, a beach bum or a sports fanatic? The answer will influence your choice of resort. A Greek island, for example, is ideal for those who want to spend two weeks roasting on the beach, but if you want to get to grips with the country's archaeological remains you need to select carefully. The Greeks have dealt quite harshly with their heritage and in many places there is really nothing left to see. Only a few of the islands – notably Crete, Corfu and Rhodes – will have what you are looking for. If you want a lively nightlife you are almost certain to be in luck because the Greeks are very good at providing entertainment late into the night. But if you need your eight hours' sleep you must choose your destination with care or you will be kept awake by the sound of partying well into the small hours.

Michael Palin

Since his days as a member of the Monty Python team, Michael Palin has made a new name for himself by taking on several epic journeys to various parts of the world. He didn't begin his travelling career until he was in his mid-forties, and in 2004, at the age of 61, he is still going strong with his Himalaya series on the BBC. Over the years he has completed a modern version of *Around the World in Eighty Days*, has travelled from pole to pole, and has explored the Sahara desert. His good humour and infectious enthusiasm have made him even more popular than ever. He comes across as an ordinary traveller whose feats, though impressive, we might be able to emulate.

INSURANCE

Setting out on any holiday without first arranging some travel insurance is inviting trouble. While you travel you are always at risk of illness, accident, theft or other disasters. These things are quite distressing enough in themselves but are made many times worse if you also find yourself lumbered with huge bills to pay.

Shopping for travel insurance can be a dispiriting business, but it has to be done. The best way to do it is to go on the internet and start comparing the deals on offer; visit, for instance, www.rapidinsure.co.uk and www.insuresupermarket.com. (If you prefer a more personal approach, there are plenty of agencies that can help you – just look under 'Insurance' in the *Yellow Pages*.) This is easy enough, and there is no shortage of low-cost policies on offer. The problem comes when you start reading the small print. You really have to make sure you know exactly what your policy covers, and, just as important, what it does not cover. The cheapest deal often turns out to be inadequate for your needs. If you are going anywhere or planning an activity that is even remotely dangerous, for example, look carefully to see that you are covered. Insurance companies are not at all keen on anything that smacks of risk and you will probably find that if you have your heart set on an adventure it will be more difficult and more expensive to get adequate cover.

Incidentally, this also applies to car hire. If you want to hire a car in one country and then drive it through other countries in western Europe, that's usually fine; but if you intend to visit former Soviet bloc countries you need to make sure that the hire company's terms and conditions allow this. Those companies that do allow you to visit eastern Europe will probably slap on a surcharge to cover what they deem to be the extra risk. They also add conditions designed to minimise their liability, for example by stipulating that the car should always be parked in a proper car park. Some of these conditions can be difficult to meet, so plan carefully and be aware of potential untoward scenarios.

Many companies offer a policy that will cover you for multiple journeys for a whole year. If you intend to do some serious travelling you might save yourself time and expense by taking one of these.

LANGUAGE BARRIERS

Your preparations for your holiday could also involve learning to speak at least some of the local language – the first way to make a good impression, for the British are notorious for their inability to speak in a foreign tongue. As long as you stick to the big resorts where thousands of other Brits take their holidays you'll find that waiters, bar staff, taxi drivers and so on speak English; but if you stray even a short distance from these areas you will find that the habitual 'Do you speak English?' is mostly met with blank stares. And if you want to go right off the beaten track then you can forget about finding English speakers to smooth your path. So why not learn some of the local language?

To some Brits this seems a completely outrageous suggestion. Surely if you speak slowly and loudly they *must* understand. No, I'm afraid they don't. So you either learn some of their language or you have numerous frustrating encounters where you can't make yourself understood.

Beginners' classes in all the major European languages are included in the prospectuses of most adult education pro- grammes (see 'Training and education' on page 71). If you take a class in the autumn, just think how well you'll be able to commu- nicate by the following summer. You don't have to be fluent, and it really is easy to pick up enough words and phrases to get by. You will also benefit from a strong psychological effect: if the people you meet feel you have made an effort to communicate they'll be much more inclined to help. Just imagine how you would feel if a tourist came up to you and asked for directions in Italian!

> Bashfulness is an ornament to youth, but a reproach to old age.
>
> *Aristotle*

Once you have some knowledge of a language it can come in handy in all sorts of situations, even in countries where that lan- guage isn't spoken. For example, many years ago I was sent to Israel on business and had to find an address in the ultra- orthodox area of Jerusalem. Naturally I got lost, but eventually I found myself walking along in step with a Jewish man of about my own age. I didn't know any Hebrew. Yes, I know what you're think- ing: I should have taken my own advice and learnt some before I went there. That is one of the reasons I now advocate learning the local language. However, I soon found that my companion spoke Yiddish, which is so close to German that it is quite comprehensi- ble. My wife is German so I have a working knowledge of the language. Using this German/Yiddish mixture he was able to give me directions that put me back on the right path.

If you really don't have the time or energy to learn a language you can at least take a phrasebook with you and learn common expressions. Even if you can only say 'hello', 'goodbye', 'please' and 'thank you', it will look as if you're making an effort.

LOCAL CUSTOMS

Once you abandon organised guided tours you will have to deal with the local population without the help of a guide. If you are to get on with them well you must have some idea about local cus- toms, for it can be easy to give offence without meaning to. For example, throughout much of the Far East it is the height of rudeness to enter a house with your shoes on; do it in a temple or mosque and you will cause grave offence. The world is full of customs that may look strange to us but which will land you in bother if you fail to observe them. In Islamic countries there are rules about female modesty that vary from being fairly lax to extremely severe. You may think that this is a terrible affront to the dignity of women, but as a guest in the country you have to stick to the rules or you face the possibility not just of being told off but of being arrested and jailed.

When I taught English in Thailand I was surprised to learn about the enormous respect in which the Thais hold their royal family. It was a far cry from the sort of treatment the royals often receive in the UK. While I was there another Englishman made the mistake of saying something derogatory about the king. The idiot thought it was a joke, but when he found himself arrested and jailed he realised that no one else shared his sense of humour. He was eventually deported after paying a very hefty fine.

On a lighter note, I was in a Thai restaurant when four British businessmen came in and ordered lunch. They were mortified to be offered spoons with which to eat, and demanded chopsticks. There was a lot of fuss and muttering, but eventually the chopsticks were produced and the men got on with their meal, blissfully unaware that the Thais, who always eat with a spoon, had had to send out to a local Chinese restaurant to procure the chopsticks.

HOLIDAYS FOR OLDIES

We can't really discuss holidays for the over fifties without mentioning Saga. The company has specialised in holidays for older travellers since just after World War Two, and now it is a household name forever associated with the more mature traveller.

Younger people may imagine that Saga is all about ancient holidaymakers being taken on dull holidays to places full of other geriatrics, but the truth could not be more different. Saga have been very quick to catch on to the idea of active oldies who want excitement and adventure in glamorous destinations. A quick look at their website (www.saga.co.uk) will give you an idea of the huge variety of holidays for all tastes on offer. There is a 'Borneo Rainforest Adventure', 'The Wonders of Vietnam', a trip to the Verona Opera Festival, or for those who want something less taxing a short break in one of the many Hilton hotels dotted around the UK.

Why would you want to go with Saga? Apart from the fact that they have half a century of experience helping older people to enjoy holidays, there is also the fact that all their customers have to be 50 or older. Some people will feel much more at home in a group where they can be sure there will be no noisy children or truculent teens to disturb them. They will also be reassured that the people they meet are likely to be those with whom they have something in common.

Furthermore, some people like to have all the hard work of organising a holiday done for them. It is quite comforting to know that all you have to do is turn up on the right day and all your travel arrangements, hotel reservations and so on will have been taken care of. You can just sit back and relax.

> A graceful and honourable old age is the childhood of immortality.
>
> *Pindar*

Another attraction is that because many older people are on their own they welcome the chance to meet others in the same situation. On a Saga holiday you are very likely to come across other single people who will ensure that you don't feel lonely while you're away. And, who knows, you might even pull.

To be fair, Saga is not the only provider of holidays for older people. If this is the sort of holiday for you, then you could also contact:

- Shearings Holidays Ltd, Miry Lane, Wigan WN3 4AG (tel: 01942 824824; website: www.shearingsholidays.com)
- Wallace Arnold Tours, 62 George Street, Croydon, Surrey CR9 1DN (tel: 020 8688 7255 or 020 8686 2378; website: www.waworldchoice.com)

THE BIG ADVENTURE

Because travelling to far-off places is getting easier there are plenty of people eager to experience a holiday that involves true adventure in some of the really wild places of the world. Too often, however, their enthusiasm outweighs their ability or even their common sense. If any of what follows strikes you as too obvious to be worth saying, then skip it. But it has been included precisely because every year many people die needlessly on such expeditions.

For some people seem unable to understand that a journey through, say, the Australian outback is different from a Sunday-afternoon stroll in Surrey. Getting really lost in the UK is so hard as to verge on the impossible – except, perhaps, in extreme weather conditions. I once took my family on a walk through Thetford Forest in Norfolk. It isn't even a proper forest; it's just an area of conifers grown for the timber industry. The paths are all well maintained and clearly marked. You are probably never more than a few miles from the visitor centre. What could possibly go wrong? It was a lovely morning in early spring and we were enjoying a pleasant stroll when, right out of nowhere, a blizzard struck up. In a couple of minutes we were struggling along paths that now seemed confusing and unfamiliar. We could hardly see where we were going because the snow was getting into our eyes. My son called out, 'I'm only eight – I'm too young to die!' We've teased him about it since, but at the time no one was laughing. Fortunately we stumbled upon the path that led to the visitor centre and managed to take shelter there.

> It is a mistake to regard age as a downhill grade toward dissolution. The reverse is true. As one grows older, one climbs with surprising strides.
>
> *George Sand*

My point is, if you can face disaster in a place as unthreatening as Thetford Forest, there is nowhere you should think of as completely safe. And some other countries are a lot more forbidding than Thetford Forest. They contain vast expanses of wood, wilderness or desert where if you get lost no one will ever see you again. If you want a really graphic account of how such a thing can happen you should read Bill Bryson's book *A Walk in the Woods*, in which he describes his hike along the Appalachian Trail. Needless to say, before you trek through really wild country you need to be fully prepared.

KNOWLEDGE

Read up as much as you can about the area you're going to visit. Find out what dangers you may encounter and what you can do about them. Are there poisonous snakes? If so, what sort? And what do you do if you get bitten? Can you take stocks of anti-venom with you? What happens, for example, if you encounter a grizzly bear? If you are going to an area where you might encounter bears it would be a very good idea indeed to find out how to avoid them. There are endless possible dangers when crossing wild country so you need to talk to people who know the area well and who can give you good advice.

EXERCISE

It would make sense to build up your stamina before you start on a long trek. If you suddenly find yourself lugging 40lb on a testing cross-country route you might find that your body is not up to the strain. Of course, as you continue your trek you will get stronger and fitter, but even so it would be a good idea to do at least a few test walks before you set out for real. Try a few miles in hilly country while carrying some kit and see how you get on. If you have boots that pinch or a rucksack that rubs your back raw, you need to know that before you start trekking for real.

CLOTHING AND EQUIPMENT

You must dress for all weather conditions you might meet on the way, so think about what you should pack. Just because you start out on a beautiful sunny day, don't be fooled into thinking that it will stay that way. It is surprising how suddenly the weather can change – as I found out that day in Thetford Forest – and when it does, you don't want to get caught with inadequate clothing. And once you're sure you have the right clothing, what about equipment?

- If you're going to sleep outside you need a proper tent that is robust enough to stand up to really bad weather. You also need to be able to erect it quickly and efficiently before you start out. Make sure that you have a drill for making camp and that every member of your expedition knows what they are supposed to do. If you have to make camp quickly in bad weather it is hardly the right time to sort out who does what.

- The thing you really need is water. You can do without food for quite some time, but without water you're in big trouble. It's heavy to carry, so if there are rivers and streams along the way you should carry only as much as you need to get to the next stop. But if you're using water from streams you need to take purification tablets. The water may look inviting and may taste fine, but you don't know what could be lurking in it.

- Learn to use a map and compass to navigate. This isn't at all easy if you haven't done it before. You should take a bit of time before your trip to practise in some less threatening countryside. The most common mistake people make is to look at the landscape in front of them and, using their imagination, make it fit the map they have. Sounds stupid? Yes, but it is done all the time. You really need to look closely at the map and make sure that it corresponds *exactly* with the view in front of you. If it doesn't you need to find out where you went wrong. Saying 'Oh, it'll probably be OK if we go this way' is really not a good idea. Once you lose the connection between your actual route and the route on the map it will be one hell of a job to find it again.

- You need to take a good first-aid kit and know how to use it. A course in basic first aid would be a very good idea. It all looks very easy when they do it on TV hospital soaps but in real life it can be quite different, especially if someone is busy bleeding to death. Knowing exactly what to do and practising the drill regularly make a lot of sense.

GETTING LOST

Before you go anywhere you should make sure that someone knows where you are going and when you expect to arrive. If you bother to take this simple precaution then if anything goes wrong at least the rescue service will have an idea where to start looking for you.

There are a few simple things you need to do if you get lost. Once again they are so obvious that you wouldn't think it worth mentioning, but, as before, people regularly fail to do them and die as a result.

- If you are with a boat, airplane or vehicle then stay with it if at all possible. It is much easier for a rescuer in a plane to spot large objects than people.
- Rescuers will search for you using infra-red sensing equipment that looks for body heat. However, a human can easily be mistaken for an animal, therefore it is necessary to generate more heat.
- If it is possible to do so safely you should light a fire and keep it going day and night. The problem with such a fire is that it needs a large amount of fuel and you might not be able to find enough. You can get small, portable stoves that burn much less wood and produce a greater amount of heat. From above they look like beacons and could attract the attention of rescuers.
- Unless you are adept at making fire by rubbing two sticks together (and who is?), you need some matches in a waterproof wrapping.
- It is important to keep warm and dry. If there are several of you, then huddle together and share your body heat.
- Carry extra food and water in case you get lost. As soon as it is clear that you have a problem, start to ration your supplies.
- You should have a torch with you, some spare batteries and a couple of spare bulbs.
- A good-quality multi-purpose knife is always useful.
- In hot weather, make sure you have sunglasses and sunscreen. In snowy conditions, you may need goggles to protect your eyes from the glare.

A WELL-KEPT SECRET

If you don't feel up to really adventurous holidays, it is still possible to get away from it all without going to the ends of the earth. Currently, one of the best-kept travel secrets is eastern Europe, which is an excellent place to explore and enjoy new experiences.

The British never really had much connection with this area in the past, and since the death of the Soviet empire we have not hurried to make contact with these countries. Many people still experience feelings of unease at the thought of visiting a country that was until only recently hidden behind the Iron Curtain.

First of all, there's the matter of language. The languages of eastern Europe are so utterly different from ours that you can't even begin to guess at what most of the signs say. Some countries even use the Cyrillic alphabet, which looks even more intimidating. But don't let these little problems bother you. In the first place many people will be able to get by in at least one Western language, so you will often find that a bit of English, German or even Italian will get you a very long way. Secondly, though Slavic languages are hell to learn properly, it is quite possible to learn enough bits and pieces from a phrasebook to get you through most situations.

The other fact that has not quite penetrated yet is that these countries have all travelled a very long way in a remarkably short time. Most of them are now parliamentary democracies with cities and towns that are as modern and up to date as anything we have in the West, and just as historic. If you feel that you are about to become an extra in a scene from *Doctor Zhivago*, relax. It really isn't like that any more.

A really useful website is www.all-holiday-brochures.com, which will send you all the holiday brochures for eastern Europe and other places around the world you could ever need, and saves you the trouble of visiting endless travel agents and lugging brochures around town.

> Greatness is the dream of youth realised in old age.
> *Alfred Victor Vigny*

OTHER ACTIVITY HOLIDAYS

Do you fancy a holiday devoted to diving, playing golf, learning Italian cookery or attending Formula One races? If so, you can enjoy all these and more by contacting Holiday Wizard Ltd, PO Box 871, Guildford GU2 4ZP (tel: 01306 877145, UK office hours only; email: wizard@holidaywizard.co.uk; website: www.holidaywizard.co.uk).

HOLIDAY HEALTH

Holidays are supposed to be a time for rest, relaxation and making yourself feel good about life. But for far too many people they end up being the cause of some sort of illness. Many of these problems are avoidable with a little forethought.

The simple act of going abroad can be enough to make your body lodge a protest. The moment it finds itself being supplied with different food and different air, the body starts to wonder what is going on. If you want to avoid problems you have to treat your body with some respect. Don't start your holiday by making radical changes to your normal diet. Especially, don't start the holiday by bingeing on cheap local booze.

The thing everybody fears most on holiday is picking up a stomach bug and having to spend some of your valuable time chained to the loo. Nothing is so effective at turning your dream holiday into a living nightmare. Happily, standards of hygiene in many of our favourite holiday destinations have improved drastically in recent years, and places that once welcomed the tourist with a delicate whiff of raw sewage are now clean and safe. Even so, you would be wise to take precautions.

- Wash your hands before touching food.
- If you are in any doubt about the local water, stick to bottled mineral water (and make sure you use it for cleaning your teeth as well). When buying water, make sure it is genuine branded mineral water with an unbroken seal. It is not unknown for bottles filled with tap water to be sold to unsuspecting tourists. If you have ice in your drinks you must make sure that it was made from bottled water. Fortunately, water supplies throughout Europe are much safer than they used to be, but if in doubt it is better to be safe than sorry.
- Don't eat any meat that has not been thoroughly cooked and is still hot. If it has been left standing around, don't touch it.
- Eat only fruit that can be peeled or cooked. Vegetables also need to be thoroughly cooked. Don't touch salads unless you have made them yourself.
- Shellfish is often advertised as a local delicacy, but you need to bear in mind that even thorough cooking can't kill off all the toxins it may contain.

- Look out for food that could have been contaminated by flies.
- It is not always possible to spot which restaurants and cafés are serious about hygiene, but it is dead easy to spot the ones that couldn't care less. Don't take a chance – eat somewhere else.
- Swimming in water contaminated with sewage is a common way to pick up bugs. Only swim in places where you are sure that the water is safe.

If you are planning something really adventurous, you must take extra precautions. First, you need to find out what diseases are endemic to the regions you are visiting and make sure you have all the inoculations you need. Most people are savvy enough to have the obvious jabs like typhoid and cholera, but it is easy to forget to check that your tetanus jab is up to date and that you are fully protected against polio. If you are going to an area where malaria is common you need to start taking the pills before you get there.

BON VOYAGE!

Don't let all the above warnings and cautions put you off! A really adventurous holiday is a great thrill and something you will remember for the rest of your life. It is well worth all the planning and effort. If you just take sensible precautions and do a bit of research and preparation it is very likely that the whole holiday will pass without incident. And if anything does go wrong it is probable that the precautions you have taken will be enough to save you from anything worse than a little inconvenience.

Three

Health and Well-being

Having reached later middle age it really is time to make some hard decisions about your health. By this stage in their lives many people are overweight, some drink more than is good for them, and some have not been able to give up smoking. These are habits you may have had for many years, and consequently they are very hard to break. But you have a tough choice to make: either you work on your bad habits and conquer them, or you carry on as you are and accept the consequences. And make no mistake – some of the consequences can be dire.

> After 30, a body has a mind of its own.
>
> *Bette Midler*

SMOKING

On average, smokers die ten years younger than non-smokers. Think of what those extra years would mean to you and your family. Smoking will:

- greatly increase your chance of developing lung cancer;
- increase your chances of having a heart attack;
- make you short of breath;
- give you a nasty cough;
- make you prone to attacks of bronchitis;
- make you vulnerable to lung diseases such as emphysema;
- make your skin look old and give you what is known as a 'smoker's face';
- make your breath, clothes and hair stink.

And if the cost of all of the above is not enough to sway you, work out what smoking is costing you in terms of money every week, every month, every year. You could even work out how much money you've spent on tobacco products since you started smoking. If you're 60 and you've been smoking a packet of cigarettes a day for 40 years, even allowing for the fluctuations in price you've willingly parted with over £25,000.

If you make an effort now to give up you will be doing yourself a favour that will last you the rest of your life. On the other hand, you might agree with the fictional barrister Horace Rumpole when he said, 'There's no pleasure on earth that's worth sacrificing for the sake of an extra five years in the geriatric ward of the Sunset Old People's Home, Weston-Super-Mare.' The choice is yours.

GIVING UP

If you're a smoker you probably get fed up with people nagging you to give up. But the fact is that by smoking you are chopping up to *ten years* off your life expectancy. That is an awful lot of time to give up for the sake of a bad habit. Even if you have smoked since you were young, giving up now will improve your chances of living longer.

> One of the many pleasures of old age is giving things up.
> *Malcolm Muggeridge*

Those of us who have smoked know just how hard it is to quit. That nicotine rush you get from the first smoke of the day is very seductive. As is the case with overeating, people who smoke have a variety of complicated psychological reasons for their habit. Looked at dispassionately, smoking looks like a pretty disgusting habit. You set light to a bunch of old leaves and breathe in the resulting fumes. Ugh! Only it isn't that simple. Smoking helps people deal with their problems, helps them to relax, and gives them a common bond with their fellow smokers. These are all good reasons to continue with the habit. As if that were not enough we also have the problem that nicotine is powerfully addictive, and attempting to give it up produces a number of unpleasant symptoms.

IT'S TOO LATE FOR ME

Older people who smoke usually come up with a predictable range of excuses. 'It's too late to stop at my time of life' is a common one; 'I simply couldn't manage without a cigarette' is another. And then, of course, there is the old favourite: 'Well, you've got to die of *something*, haven't you?'

First, it is never too late to give up. Even the health of people who have smoked for 30 or 40 years will improve after quitting. The body's repair mechanism is a remarkable thing, and once you stop it will get to work. And once the withdrawal symptoms have ceased, you will start to feel better. You don't realise it because you have been smoking for so long, but actually you are constantly feeling slightly unwell as a result of your habit. When you quit and your system can rid itself of the nicotine and carbon monoxide, you will feel brighter and more energetic. Moreover, after ten to fifteen years of giving up, an ex-smoker's chances of developing lung cancer are only slightly higher than those of someone who has never smoked.

AIDS TO GIVING UP

These days there are many ways of giving up, but all of them, of course, require a degree of willpower.

- Nicotine replacement
  Patches, which come in various sizes and strengths, can be applied to the skin and release a measured dose of nicotine into the bloodstream. As the treatment proceeds the amount of nicotine released decreases until at last you have been weaned off the addiction. There is also nicotine gum to chew, and an inhaler that looks like a cigarette through which you can breathe in a dose of nicotine.

- Hypnotherapy
  A hypnotherapist will put you into a light trance and then plant a positive suggestion that will help you give up your habit post-hypnosis. You can either find a therapist who will treat you individually (they are listed in the *Yellow Pages*), or sometimes you can find therapists who conduct a session with a roomful of people. You might find that being together with people who share your problem is helpful. I must admit to being quite sceptical about this technique until one of my friends who had been a heavy smoker for years tried it and never smoked again from that day onwards.

- Acupuncture
  This is an ancient Chinese remedy that involves inserting needles into various parts of the body. The Chinese believe that a type of energy called chi flows along invisible meridians within the body, and that inserting needles into points along these meridians allows the chi to be redirected to areas where it is most needed. For the purpose of helping people to give up smoking most acupuncturists don't use needles but instead rely on a small stud that is taped to part of the body, usually the ear lobe. When you feel the urge to smoke you press the stud lightly and your craving will subside. This is another technique that once aroused my scepticism, but again I know of someone who rid himself of a heavy smoking habit through acupuncture.

But as I said, for any of these methods, and others, to work, you must *really* want to be rid of the habit. This sounds obvious, but if you have ever weaned yourself off a bad habit you'll know that there were many times when in theory you wanted to quit but in practice you simply didn't have the willpower. Then there comes a day when you suddenly find you have the energy and commitment to conquer your cravings. Whenever you find yourself at one of these junctures in life you must grab the opportunity and not let go.

FURTHER INFORMATION

- For those who want to quit smoking, try Dr Bob's Quit Smoking Page, an American website that has loads of good advice for would-be quitters; visit unr.edu/homepage/shubinsk/smoke.html.
- If you want to talk to others who are trying to give up the evil weed, try the newsgroup at www.swen.uwaterloo.ca/~as3/as3.html.

Albert Schweitzer

Born in 1875, Schweitzer, who came from a deeply religious family, began his career by studying theology and intended to devote his life to religion. However, later on he decided that he wanted to be a medical missionary, which meant that at the relatively old age of 30 he had to commence a long and difficult medical training. He eventually received his MD, and in 1913 he founded a hospital at Lambaréné in French Equatorial Africa. In 1917 he and his wife were sent to a French internment camp as prisoners of war, but were released the next year. Schweitzer then spent six years in Europe, but in 1924 he returned to Lambaréné, and this was the place where he chose to spend the rest of his life. At Lambaréné, he was not only doctor and surgeon in the hospital, but also found time to serve as pastor of the congregation and administrator of a village. He also pursued an active writing career and never gave up the music for which he had become famous. He was inundated with honours for his work and eventually received the Nobel Peace Prize in 1952, at the age of 77. He used the prize money to open a treatment centre for lepers in Lambaréné. Schweitzer died in 1965.

OBESITY

You would have had to be lost in a desert somewhere not to have heard the news that being overweight has a bad effect on your health. The message is being pumped out by the media virtually every day. Most of us are well aware that we should lose at least some weight, but as the years go by we just keep getting fatter and fatter.

> The great secret that all old people share is that you really haven't changed in 70 or 80 years. Your body changes, but you don't change at all. And that, of course, causes great confusion.
>
> *Doris Lessing*

As with smoking, the damage done by excess weight is no mystery. You do not have to be a medical expert to understand that excess poundage:

- increases your chances of developing high blood pressure;
- increases your chances of developing heart disease;
- increases your chances of developing diabetes;
- increases your chances of contracting cancer;
- makes it harder for you to take exercise (and the inactivity results in your putting on even more weight);
- makes you look older and less attractive.

Knowing all these things, however, is not the same as doing anything about the problem.

LOSING WEIGHT

Millions of people would like to lose weight but find themselves unable to do so. A vast industry has been built on the back of this problem. There is a constant stream of diets, treatments, pills, potions and exercise regimes all of which claim to help you lose weight and to keep it off permanently.

What makes losing weight so hard is that the battle is never really over. Losing some weight is not that hard, and most of us have succeeded at some point in getting rid of part of our excess baggage. There is a sense of achievement about losing weight that helps us to conquer our cravings for food. But once we get down to our target weight, what then? The battle continues day in, day out for the rest of our lives. People who give up a bad habit like smoking (see above) at least have the satisfaction that after a long struggle they can actually congratulate themselves on having conquered it. They get to a point where they don't even want to smoke, and eventually they find tobacco smoke repugnant. But you can't give up food, and it's therefore easier to slide back into your old habits.

> Experience is simply the name we give our mistakes.
> *Oscar Wilde*

We overeat for many reasons. Some people find comfort in eating and make it one of the ways in which they deal with the stresses of everyday life. Having a bad day at the office? A bar of chocolate can provide solace. Perversely, the opposite also happens: many people will have a snack to reward themselves for having done well. Some of us use food as a way of escaping boredom, as part of the rituals of socialising with our friends, or as a way of relaxing after a period of stress. In short, we can always think of a 'good' reason for a snack. Another problem is that we are always drawn to the foods that are bad for us. Given a choice between a piece of chocolate and a raw carrot, which would you choose? No contest! So we are faced with a situation in which we constantly crave the very foods that are going to damage our health the most.

If we were all sensible, rational creatures, there would be no weight problems. But the truth is that we are not rational and our motives are often complicated and have their roots deep in our unconscious. Even so, there is no real mystery about losing weight: simply cut out sweet, fatty foods, eat more fresh fruit and vegetables, and take more exercise. How has an industry worth billions of dollars been built on the back of such skimpy facts? The answer is that no one likes that advice very much and they therefore look for easy, painless ways of achieving their aim. Sadly, there aren't any. But there are some things you can do that will help you to make the necessary effort.

- Keep a diary of *everything* you eat over the course of a couple of weeks. If you are completely honest with yourself you'll soon see where the excess calories are coming from.
- Don't attempt to make sweeping changes to your diet. If you do you'll only suffer terrible cravings and will soon start eating too much again. Go instead for small, sustainable changes. For example, if you are in the habit of having a chocolate bar with your mid-morning coffee, substitute a piece of fruit. You won't enjoy the fruit as much, but it is only a small change and it shouldn't require much willpower to keep it up. Using your diary, you can then identify all the things you eat that are contributing to your weight problem and cut them out one by one, at the same time introducing more healthy foods into your diet.
- Drinking plenty of water will help to ease your cravings for excess food. Medical advice is that we should all drink two litres of water every day. This is a lot to get through, but you will find that if you keep a glass of water by you while you work and keep taking sips throughout the day it will help you to do without snacks.
- It always helps if you can identify the reasons why you overeat. Are you using snacks as a way of dealing with stress or boredom, or are you in the habit of rewarding yourself with food for a job well done? If you can understand why you keep snacking you have a greater chance of tackling it and stopping it.

The good news is that after a while your body will adjust to the new regime and your stomach will stop telling you that you're hungry when you're not. Eventually, eating healthily will become a matter of habit.

But beware – the habit of overeating is never completely defeated. There will be times when your emotions are upset and you will be tempted to respond by eating more to make you feel better.

Even if you give in occasionally – and you probably will – you need to make an effort to return to your sensible habits straight away. If you've put in hard work it would be tragic to give up now, but this is what happens to many people who have lost weight. Just like the members of Alcoholics Anonymous, you must learn to conquer your habit one day at a time.

FURTHER INFORMATION

For advice about losing weight, try the following:

- Weight Watchers UK Ltd, Customer Services Department, Millennium House, Ludlow Road, Maidenhead, Berkshire SL6 2SL (website: www.weightwatchers.co.uk).
- Weightlossforgood has all the information and help you need at www.weightlossforgood.co.uk.
- Patient UK is another site for those hoping to lose weight; go to www.patient.co.uk.
- If you think that hypnosis might help, you can try Oxford Hypnotherapy (tel: 01993 778622; email: enquiries@hypnos.info; website: www.hypnos.info).

THE DEMON DRINK

Alcohol is one of the few toxic substances that actually possess the ability to persuade us that we need more and more of it. Drinking is such a well-established part of our culture that we think of it as a pleasant social activity; it never occurs to us to regard it as a form of drug taking. It is the acceptability of drinking alcohol that has made it so dangerous. Almost everyone drinks, and many people drink far more than is good for them, but because we live in an alcohol-friendly culture it is quite acceptable to get drunk. Nowadays there is a well-established culture of binge-drinking which is prevalent in all age groups and all social classes. At weekends, hospital A&E departments are full of people who have been injured in fights or accidents fuelled by excess alcohol.

Older people are not the worst offenders when it comes to bad behaviour involving alcohol, but that does not mean that they drink wisely. It is not at all hard to drink too much without ever being seriously drunk or behaving disgracefully. And alcohol does have serious effects on the body:

- It is high in calories and will make it hard for you to maintain a healthy weight.
- Over time, alcohol will cause your blood pressure to rise.
- Too much alcohol increases your chances of contracting various cancers.
- Too much alcohol increases your chances of suffering from Type 2 diabetes.
- Too much alcohol increases your chances of contracting cirrhosis of the liver.
- Too much alcohol increases your chances of having an accident.

There is, of course, no need to give up drinking altogether. In fact, as most people now know, a glass or two of red wine every day is regarded as being quite beneficial. The trick is to drink in moderation – which is harder than it sounds, because however good your intentions may be, when you start drinking they are likely to be undermined by the effects of the alcohol. Unfortunately, the alcohol consumption the medical profession regards as sensible falls somewhat short of the amount most people would like to drink:

- Men should drink no more than 21 units of alcohol per week (and no more than four units in any one day).
- Women should drink no more than 14 units of alcohol per week (and no more than three units in any one day).

One unit of alcohol is 10ml (1cl) by volume, or 8g by weight, of pure alcohol. So, for example:

- A half-pint of average-strength beer, cider or lager (up to 5% alcohol by volume) contains one unit.
- A small pub measure (25ml) of spirits (40% alcohol by volume) contains one unit; a standard pub measure (35ml) of spirits contains one and a half units.
- A standard pub measure of fortified wine such as sherry or port (20 % alcohol by volume) contains one unit.
- A small glass (125ml) of average-strength wine (12% alcohol by volume) contains one and a half units.

The medical advice is that you should drink a little each day rather than a lot all at once. You are also supposed to have a couple of alcohol-free days a week to give your liver a chance to recover.

> Age does not depend upon years, but upon temperament and health. Some men are born old, and some never grow so.
>
> *Tryon Edwards*

All this self-denial is rather hard to take. Some people take the view that if they can't drink – or eat, or smoke – to their heart's content then they might just as well be dead. It is their right to think this, but it will be no good regretting it when ill health strikes. The old 'you have to die of something' argument is deeply flawed. Of course all of us will die at some point, but if you are sensible about your health now you might be six feet under when you're 85 rather than 70, and for many of those extra years you will have been untroubled by serious health problems.

If you get to grips with your lifestyle now, you will be able to remain 'middle-aged' until well into your old age. It's a prize worth fighting for. To be able to enjoy life fully into your seventies, eighties and even nineties is by no means impossible, but it will take an effort on your part.

FURTHER INFORMATION

- If your life is adversely affected by alcohol you can get help and information from Alcohol Concern, Waterbridge House, 32–36 Loman Street, London SE1 0EE (tel: 020 7928 7377; website: www.alcoholconcern.org.uk/).
- If you feel that you need help to give up alcohol altogether you can contact Alcoholics Anonymous at General Service Office of AA, PO Box 1, Stonebow House, Stonebow, York Y01 7NJ (tel: 01904 644026; website: www.alcoholics-anonymous.org.uk).
- If a member of your family is an alcoholic you can get help from Al-Anon, an organisation that specialises in the problems of families affected by alcoholism. Contact them at Al-Anon Family Groups UK & Eire, 61 Great Dover Street, London SE1 4YF (tel: 020 7403 0888; website: www.al-anonuk.org.uk/).

CARING FOR YOUR TEETH, EYES AND EARS

TEETH

One of the great miseries of old age has always been the loss of one's teeth. To our parents' generation this was seen as an inevitable part of the ageing process and the only thing you could do about it was to get the best set of dentures you could afford. Even now a lack of oral hygiene has made Britain infamous in other countries, especially the US, where expensive dental care is a priority for those who can afford it.

If you are in any doubt about just how bad the situation is, make a point of noticing the teeth of anybody over 40. Depressingly, often it is not a pretty sight. There are several factors that contribute to this situation:

- First, dental hygiene has never been a great priority for the British. They are constantly urged by health advisers and toothpaste commercials to take good care of their teeth, but this advice is seldom heeded.
- Second, our diet is such that the teeth are under constant attack. We eat far too much sweet stuff, and if you regularly bathe your teeth in a sugary solution you are just asking for damage to your teeth and gums.
- Finally, it is increasingly hard to get an NHS dentist, and private dentistry is very expensive. All this has led to a situation where far too many people only go near a dentist when they can't bear the pain any more.

A recent ad aiming to encourage better dental hygiene bore the slogan 'Ignore your teeth and they'll go away'. How true that is, and many people, including some dentists, still regard the loss of teeth as inevitable. My former dentist told me when I was in my early thirties, 'You'll probably lose all your teeth by the time you're 40.' He made it sound as if that was a natural state of affairs and nothing much to worry about. But I had already seen the sheer misery my parents had endured with dentures. All those TV ads that show merry, smiling people who, as long as they use the right fixative, can lead jolly lives eating whatever they like are sheer piffle. Dentures are bad news. Fortunately I got myself a new dentist with a less fatalistic approach and, apart from the loss of a couple of wisdom teeth, I still have a full set even though I'm now over 50.

> All would live long, but none would be old.
> *Benjamin Franklin*

But the change was not brought about by magic or even by any kind of scientific miracle; it was simply down to being taught how to look after my teeth properly. I had always thought that I was doing a good job of cleaning my teeth. I never forgot to give them a vigorous brushing night and morning. I genuinely felt I was doing my bit. The fact that I regularly needed fillings was something of a mystery to me. I assumed that cavities in teeth just happened and there wasn't much I could do about it. Fortunately for me, my new dentist had other ideas. He packed me off to see a dental hygienist who made me go through my tooth-cleaning drill and then told me quite bluntly that I wasn't anywhere near thorough enough. This is how you should do it:

- Use a soft-bristled brush. Synthetic bristles are better than natural bristles, which harbour bacteria because they are more porous. The brush also needs to be the right size. Generally, smaller brushes are much better than large ones.
- Hold the brush so that the bristles are at a 45-degree angle to the teeth. Make sure you push the tips of the bristles into the space under the gums.
- Brush gently so that any plaque growing under the gums is removed. Plaque is very sticky stuff, almost like glue, so to get rid of it requires persistence.
- You need to brush the outside, the inside and the chewing surfaces of your teeth. For the front teeth you should brush the inside surfaces of the upper and lower jaws by holding the brush vertically and making numerous up and down strokes with the tip of the brush over the teeth and gums.

- Learn to brush each tooth individually. Brushing a whole group of teeth at one go does little good.
- Don't forget to brush your tongue, because it helps to freshen your breath. Bacteria and small food particles can collect on your tongue and cause bad breath.
- Brush at least twice a day, after breakfast and before bedtime. If you can manage to brush after lunch as well, so much the better.
- Don't rush the brush! You need to brush for *three minutes*. This will seem like an eternity, but that is how long it takes to do a proper job.
- Don't scrub too hard or use a hard brush because you risk damaging your gums, or even removing some of the enamel from your teeth.
- Use fluoride toothpaste because it really does help to protect your teeth from decay.
- As soon as the bristles on your brush start to spread it is time to get a new brush.
- When you have finished brushing, take some dental floss, clean out all the spaces between your teeth and have another go at the areas under the gums. You will be amazed after all that brushing just how much stuff the floss will dislodge.
- It's advisable as well to finish off by spending a few minutes gargling with an antiseptic mouthwash.
- Finally, when you first start this regime, buy some disclosing tablets. These stain any remaining plaque and show you just how thorough your brushing technique is. As the tablets will stain your mouth red or blue for some hours after you have used them, it is probably a good idea to do this just before bedtime.

As well as taking care of your teeth, you need to look carefully at your gums. If you don't clean thoroughly under the edge of the gum you risk getting gingivitis. The gums swell, turn red and bleed profusely at the slightest touch. People used to believe that this was a disease that could be caught from others and was passed around by using dirty crockery and cutlery. This is pure nonsense, but there are still some people who believe it. In fact, gingivitis is the result of letting bacteria breed unchecked under your gums. If you don't do anything about it, first the gums recede and then the disease gets into the jawbone and loosens the teeth. Then your teeth drop out. There is no point battling to keep your teeth free of cavities if you don't take really good care of your gums.

> Old age is not a disease. It is strength and survivorship, triumph over all kinds of vicissitudes and disappointments, trials and illnesses.
>
> *Maggie Kuhn*

On top of all that, you need to keep an eye on how much sugary food you eat. Bacteria love sugar as much as we do, and if your mouth is constantly awash with sugar-rich saliva it won't do your teeth and gums much good.

This probably seems an awful lot of trouble to go to, and it is. Getting into the habit of doing all this twice a day is not easy. It takes a lot of perseverance, but it is the only way to hang on to your teeth for the rest of your life.

FURTHER INFORMATION

- The British Dental Health Foundation has a website at www.dentalhealth.org.uk which offers wide-ranging advice.

EYES

Getting your eyes checked regularly becomes ever more important as you age. It is not just a matter of being able to see well, though that is important enough, for glaucoma can creep up on you unexpectedly. The condition causes increased pressure within the eyeball causing gradual loss of sight, and it is your peripheral vision that goes first so it may not be easily noticeable. Also, your optician is often able to pick up early symptoms of other diseases such as diabetes. Even brain tumours can be detected by an alert optician long before you notice symptoms that would send you to a doctor. So don't forget to have regular eye tests because they could save not just your sight but your life too.

> The spiritual eyesight improves as the physical eyesight declines.
>
> *Plato*

FURTHER INFORMATION

- RNIB Eye Health Information Service, 105 Judd Street, London WC1H 9NE (tel: 0845 766 9999; email: eyehealth@rnib.org.uk)
- RNIB Talk and Support, 105 Judd Street, London WC1H 9NE (tel: 0845 330 3723; email: talkandsupport@rnib.org.uk)
- RNIB Low Vision, 105 Judd Street, London WC1H 9NE (tel: 020 7391 2157; email: LVUeditor@rnib.org.uk)

EARS

Deafness is one of the most tiresome problems of old age. Happily, not everyone is seriously affected by the tendency of hearing to deteriorate as we age, and many older people can hear perfectly well. But for those who do have the problem it can blight their whole lives. Unfortunately, the deaf old person has become a stock comedy character, but for those who suffer from this condition there is nothing to laugh about. It is distressing because it makes communicating with those around you difficult, and it is dangerous because you are unable to hear things you need to hear, such as a smoke alarm going off.

Helen Keller

Helen Keller was born in Tuscumbia, Alabama, in 1880. She was both blind and deaf from birth, and it was thought that she would never be able to live anything but the most passive and unrewarding of lives. By the time she was seven she was frequently flying into rages of sheer frustration, and her parents decided that they needed help. So they hired a tutor named Anne Sullivan. Anne worked hard at teaching Helen to spell out words using sign language. Helen learnt the words readily enough but had no idea what they meant. Then one day at the water pump, Anne had the bright idea of holding Helen's hand under the water and spelling out W-A-T-E-R. At last she had made a breakthrough, and over the next few days Helen learned dozens of new words. By the age of ten she had learned to speak, and then she set about learning Greek, Latin, French and German in Braille. She later studied at Harvard, and during her life she wrote a dozen books, met twelve US presidents, and travelled the world. She died in 1968 at the age of 87.

It is important to look after your hearing from a young age, but there's really only one way to do it: avoid excessive noise. If you make a habit of listening to music with the volume turned right up, or if you work in a loud environment without using ear defenders, you might not notice anything at the time, but you will damage your hearing. Some men who work in noisy places think it isn't macho to take precautions to safeguard their hearing, but there is nothing macho about being as deaf as a post when you're 60.

If you haven't had your hearing tested for years, or if you suspect you have a problem such as tinnitus (a ringing in the ears), you need to have a test. It is possible that a loss of hearing is caused by nothing more serious than a build-up of wax in the ear, which can be dispersed by pouring a small amount of olive oil into the ear every day for several days. If it won't go without a fight, your doctor can syringe the ear to get rid of it.

HEARING AIDS

If your ears have suffered serious damage or if you have simply inherited a tendency to deafness, you may need a hearing aid, or, in severe cases, two aids. The aids supplied by the NHS are rather basic and large enough to be easily seen. You can buy your aid privately and you'll get a much smaller, neater unit, but at the time of writing the cost of such aids is in the region of £1,000.

The problem with hearing aids is that they increase the volume of *all* the noises around you, not just the ones you want to hear. Manufacturers are constantly claiming that they have overcome this problem and that their products will restore your hearing to something like its original state. My experience with people who have used them is that even the most expensive ones are not nearly as good as the claims, but – and this is a big but – they are much better than no aid at all.

> Few people know how to be old.
> *François de la Rochefoucauld*

LIP-READING

If all else fails, or is unsatisfactory, there are classes you can join to learn about lip-reading. Your doctor or hospital department will be able to tell you where to find the one nearest to you. Lip-reading is very effective and, so I'm told, not hard to pick up. A friend who is very deaf manages to keep up perfectly normal conversations with the help of two hearing aids and his lip-reading skills. In fact, he now copes so well that friends quite forget his deafness, unless they happen to make a remark when not facing him.

FURTHER INFORMATION

- There is a very useful article on preventing hearing problems at www.vestibular.org/prevent.html.
- Patient UK has a very useful section on self-help groups for those with hearing problems; go to www.patient.co.uk.
- The BBC has useful information for the deaf at www.bbc.co.uk/health/conditions/deafness.shtml.
- The Royal National Institute for the Deaf can be contacted on 0808 808 0123 (website: www.rnid.org.uk).

STAYING WELL

The good news is that thanks to constant advances in medical science our chances of living to an advanced age are getting better and better. What is more, we can look forward not merely to living longer but also to staying fit and active for longer. When I think of my grandparents I am amazed by how in their sixties they were already largely housebound and shuffled around looking very frail. Nobody would have considered that unusual then because it was everybody's idea of how old people should behave. But in the half-century since things have altered drastically. We are now coming to expect that people will carry on as normal well beyond 60.

> In spite of illness, in spite even of the arch enemy sorrow, one can remain alive long past the usual date of disintegration if one is unafraid of change, insatiable in intellectual curiosity, interested in big things, and happy in a small way.
>
> *Edith Wharton*

The bad news is that the reason most people live longer is largely down to improved diet and medical treatment; it has little to do with people taking better care of themselves. For reasons I have already mentioned, and more to come, it makes sense to start taking a few precautions to make sure that we live to a healthy and enjoyable old age.

BODY MAINTENANCE

If you want to live long and stay healthy the first thing to do is to rid yourself of the idea that you only attend to your body when it gives you trouble. Our whole life is a constant battle against decay.

We freeze our food, have cars serviced, weed the garden and repaint the house. All these activities are intended to slow the inevitable process of deterioration as much as possible. So why on earth do so many people view their own body as a self-perpetuating organism that will do its work faithfully and effectively without any care or maintenance whatsoever?

CHECK-UPS

Once you reach 50 you need to get yourself checked out regularly, even if you feel perfectly well. High blood pressure is very common, but because it often has no symptoms and the patient feels perfectly well it remains undiagnosed until something goes wrong. Similarly, many people have raised cholesterol levels, but as that condition too has no symptoms it won't be noticed unless you take the trouble to go to the doctor and get tested.

Supposing you don't feel well – what then? Doctors report that men frequently ignore quite serious symptoms, such as severe chest pains, on the basis that they will go away eventually. This attitude of denial is pure madness, but it is a surprisingly prevalent one. I even came across a very senior surgeon, the recently retired father of a friend, who chose to go fishing when he had chest pains on the grounds that it was 'just indigestion', and subsequently died of a heart attack. I wonder how many times he had warned patients against that sort of stupidity.

A lot is written about the lack of resources available in the NHS. We read endless news stories about people who have been unable to get much-needed medical treatment and who have spent months or years on a waiting list. That, however, is only part of the picture. If you talk to your doctor you'll discover that many people are not using the facilities available to them simply because they can't be bothered. For example, the number of people who seek treatment for high blood pressure is a tiny fraction of those who actually need it.

The trouble is that for many people going to the doctor seems to be inviting trouble. They work on the 'if it ain't broke, don't fix it' principle. This is understandable, but short-sighted. As you get older it is a safe bet that some bits of your body will no longer function as they should. If you make a habit of getting a regular check-up then early symptoms can be picked up and treatment given before your condition becomes serious.

HERBAL REMEDIES

Some people realise that they need treatment but rather than go to a doctor they rely on self-medication. You often hear people making a distinction between 'natural remedies', which are a Good Thing, and 'drugs', which are obviously a Bad Thing. I've even heard people say in all seriousness, 'Oh, it must be safe, it's only a plant.' Does it not occur to them that heroin, cocaine and cannabis are also derived from plants?

The truth about herbal remedies is that they are drugs that have not gone through the rigorous testing procedures required for real medicines. We know that the testing of medicines is not always foolproof and that there have been some terrible mistakes, but is taking remedies that have not been tested at all an answer to the problem? Enthusiasts for herbal remedies rely on the argument that these treatments have been used for hundreds of years and therefore must be safe and effective. This is not necessarily true. Because there is no monitoring process it is hard to discover just what effect these remedies have had. Also, because there are no real controls in place you can never be sure about the purity of the product you are taking, nor can you have any idea what sort of dosage you should be using.

In short, you are playing a game of Russian roulette with your health. It is far better to go to a doctor and get some proper advice. Yes, doctors and drug manufacturers do sometimes make mistakes, but they are a much better bet than the 'natural' alternative.

TAKING PILLS

One reason why people like to rely on natural remedies is that you can take them without having to admit to yourself that there is anything wrong with you. Popping a few pills made from some herb is not to many people's way of thinking the same as medication. Understandably, there is a certain resistance to the idea of taking medicines regularly. No one wants to go to the doctor feeling fine only to be told that they have raised blood pressure and that they face taking pills for the rest of their life to keep it under control. But the reality is that unless you do the right things now you are storing up trouble for yourself in the future. Taking pills to keep your heart safe is a sensible precaution, and it doesn't mean that you have suddenly become an invalid. In fact, the opposite is true: by taking medication now you are ensuring that it is far less likely you will experience serious problems later on.

SERIOUS CONDITIONS

You don't have to rush to the doctor for every minor ache, but it makes sense to get advice on anything unusual. This section covers some of the serious conditions that often get ignored until they cause real trouble. No one ever likes to think that they might get seriously ill, but the truth is that at some stage all of us will. With prompt treatment, however, many such illnesses are curable, so the advice must always be: go and see your doctor.

HEART DISEASE

Heart disease is the major killer in Europe and the US. A heart attack – technically known as a myocardial infarction – is one of the events we most fear, and sadly they are all too common. They are caused when a blood clot blocks a blood vessel in the heart, thus starving it of oxygen. This lack of oxygen will destroy part of the heart muscle, and if the damage is severe enough the heart will stop working and the patient will die. In older people the problem is often exacerbated by a narrowing of the blood vessels in the heart due to a build-up of cholesterol.

> As for me, except for an occasional heart attack I feel as young as I ever did.
>
> *Robert Benchley*

However, there are things we can do to improve our chances of not becoming ill in the first place.

- Go to see your doctor and have tests for blood pressure (BP) and cholesterol. If either is too high the doctor will probably suggest that you lose weight by sticking to a calorie-controlled low-fat diet and taking more exercise. Do it! (See 'Easy ways to stay fit' on page 136.)

- You may also be offered further tests to see whether you have any underlying problems such as diabetes or a dodgy thyroid. If you're wise you'll have these tests as well. It's easier to fix problems now than to wait until after you've had your first (and maybe final) heart attack.
- If you can't reduce your BP through exercise and diet, you will probably be offered medication. There is a range of very effective drugs that reduce BP and the doctor will choose the one that suits you best. BP-reducing drugs have to be taken for the rest of your life and many people find this upsetting because being dependent on medication seems like the first step in getting old. Try to look at it another way: by finding out that you have a problem you've done the wise thing, and by taking the tablets you've been bright enough to fix the problem.
- Similarly, high cholesterol can be treated with a family of drugs called statins. They are currently considered something of a medical miracle because not only do they reduce cholesterol, they also, by some mechanism that is not yet completely understood, have a protective effect on the heart. Some doctors go so far as to say that all adults over 50 ought to take statins. Be that as it may, if your arteries are in danger of getting bunged up with cholesterol then taking a statin is a very good idea.
- The doctor may also suggest that you take a small daily dose of aspirin. This is equivalent to a quarter of one of the tablets used for treating headaches. The aspirin thins your blood and makes clotting less likely.

If you take all these precautions then your chances of not having a heart attack are greatly increased. It may be a bit of a hassle to take pills every day, but it is far less troublesome than ignoring the problem until heart disease strikes.

SYMPTOMS

Let's assume for a moment that the worst happens and you do have a heart attack. The first thing is to know enough to recognise what is happening. Huge numbers of people have died simply because they assumed their chest pain was merely indigestion. I watched my father die for this reason, and it made me quite determined never to make the same mistake.

If you get prompt medical attention your chances of survival are good. People are increasingly going on to live healthy lives after suffering an attack. Early diagnosis is vital, and the list of symptoms that follows should help you to recognise an attack:

- a feeling of pressure, fullness or pain in the centre of the chest that lasts more than ten minutes; this may persist or it may come and go; the sensation is often described as like having an elephant sitting on your chest;
- prolonged, severe chest pain;
- pain that spreads from the chest to the shoulders, neck or arms;
- prolonged pain in the upper abdomen;
- chest discomfort accompanied by lightheadedness;
- shortness of breath, even when at rest;
- fainting;
- nausea, vomiting and/or intense sweating;
- frequent angina attacks that do not appear to be caused by exertion.

You may not experience all these symptoms, and it is even possible to suffer an attack with almost no symptoms at all, but the more your condition resembles the one described above the more likely it is that you are suffering an attack and need urgent treatment.

It is also important to know what to do when you are having a heart attack:

- Rest quietly, preferably in a sitting position.
- Take half an aspirin immediately (unless you are allergic to it).
- Sit up if breathless; lie flat if you feel faint.
- Call an ambulance.

TREATMENT

There are several treatments for heart attacks such as clot-busting drugs, balloon angioplasty (inflating a tiny balloon inside a blocked artery to reopen the passage) and coronary stenting.

These are most effective if begun very soon after the onset of symptoms. The sooner blood flow is restored, the less damage the heart will suffer and the greater your chances of making a good recovery. In the long run it may be necessary to have a coronary bypass to restore the restricted blood flow. Happily, this operation is now fairly routine and your chances of surviving it are good.

Sir Ranulph Twisleton-Wykeham-Fiennes

If Ranulph Fiennes sounds like a character out of *Boys' Own*, it is hardly surprising. His exploits sound like the work of a rather over-zealous writer of adventure fiction. He has led more than 30 expeditions to the North and South Poles, the Nile, the Arabian Desert and a host of other far-flung and almost inaccessible places. In 1982 he led the Transglobe Expedition which made the first polar circumnavigation of the globe; it took him three years to complete the 52,000 miles. There is simply not room here to detail all his remarkable exploits, but there is one story that must be told. In his late fifties Fiennes suffered a heart attack and underwent bypass surgery. Just seven months later he set out to run seven marathons on different continents one after the other. During this incredible feat even he began to doubt whether what he was attempting was possible, and at one point the press announced that he was on the verge of giving up, but he overcame his problems and finished the course. Fiennes' triumph shows us just what the human body and spirit can accomplish.

STROKE

Strokes, caused by interruptions in the blood flow towards the brain, are not easy to diagnose because the symptoms are often similar to those of other illnesses. You can, for example, be dizzy for all sorts of reasons, and most of those will be quite minor. Viral infections of facial nerves may cause numbness of the face. The big difference is that stroke symptoms tend to arrive suddenly and don't go away – although there is a condition known as transient ischaemic attack (TIA) in which a temporary blockage produces symptoms that do disappear. The trouble with TIA is that it is often a sign of more trouble to come. Over a third of people experiencing TIA will get a full-blown stroke at a later date.

SYMPTOMS

Here are the main symptoms to look out for:

- numbness or weakness of the face, arm or leg; this is particularly significant if it's only happening to one side of the body;
- confusion or fainting;
- trouble with speaking and understanding;
- blurred vision or complete loss of vision in one or both eyes;
- dizziness, trouble with walking, loss of coordination or balance;
- a bad headache, with no apparent cause.

TREATMENT

As with heart attacks, there is much that can be done to help stroke patients if you act quickly. The measures taken to prevent a stroke are precisely the same as those for preventing a heart attack. Clot-busting drugs need to be administered as soon as possible after the onset of symptoms. You should call an ambulance and make sure that you tell the emergency operator that you think you're having a stroke.

> In youth we run into difficulties; in old age difficulties run into us.
>
> *Josh Billings*

BREAST CANCER

Breast cancer is one of the diseases people frequently try to ignore. It is quite true that most lumps will turn out to be harmless cysts, but that diagnosis is not one you can make for yourself. Men assume that breast cancer is exclusively a female problem, but, though it is rare, men can contract the disease, so it is worth their also taking an interest in the warning signs.

SYMPTOMS

If you have a lump or thickening in the breast or under the arm, or if you observe any of the following symptoms, you should get to your doctor as soon as possible. Look out for:

- a clear or bloody discharge from the nipple;
- inverted nipples;
- redness or swelling;
- dimpling on the breast skin resembling the texture of an orange;
- a change in the contours of the breast, such as one being higher than the other.

A visit to the doctor will, in most cases, have the effect of putting your mind at rest. In the minority of cases where there is a genuine cause for worry, your prompt action will do a lot to improve your chances of a complete cure.

TREATMENT

Understandably enough, the reason why so many people put off getting medical advice is fear not only of the disease but of the treatment. The prospect of losing a breast and of having to endure a course of chemotherapy is terrifying. However, in many cases the treatment is extremely effective and people who have undergone it are restored to full health. So, though it is hard to admit there is a problem, it is far better than waiting until the trouble gets so bad that it can no longer be ignored.

PROSTATE PROBLEMS

Considering that it is a gland no bigger than a walnut, the prostate causes an awful lot of trouble to older men. As men get older, their prostate – which surrounds the urethra, the tube through which we urinate and ejaculate – keeps growing. As it grows, it squeezes the urethra. Since urine travels from the bladder through the urethra, the pressure from the enlarged prostate may affect bladder control. In younger men, the main problem is an inflammation called prostatitis which is often caused by bacterial infection, but once you are over 50 the most common prostate problem is prostate enlargement. Doctors call this benign prostatic hyperplasia, or BPH. Older men are at risk of contracting prostate cancer as well, but this disease is much less common than BPH.

SYMPTOMS

If you have prostate problems you may have one or more of the following symptoms:

- a frequent and urgent need to urinate; you may get up several times a night to go to the bathroom;
- trouble starting a urine stream; even though you feel you have to rush to get to the bathroom, you find it hard to start urinating;
- a weak stream of urine, or a small amount of urine each time you go;
- the feeling that you still have to go, even when you have just finished urinating;
- leaking or dribbling;
- small amounts of blood in your urine.

These symptoms may be mild, or they may make your whole life a misery. Either way they should not be ignored.

TREATMENT

The condition is treatable, and you shouldn't allow embarrassment to dissuade you from seeking help.

Suppose your worst fears are realised and it does turn out to be cancer. Prostate cancer comes in two versions: the first proceeds slowly, and it is often said that something else will kill you long before the cancer has a chance to do so; the second, however, spreads rapidly and soon infects the spine. Your chances of recovering from this one are slimmer. It used to be difficult for doctors to decide which version of the disease they were treating. However, while this book was being written there was an announcement that a test has now been devised to distinguish between the fast and slow varieties of prostate cancer.

As with most cancers, the treatment may consist of removing the offending organ and then treating the patient with radiotherapy and/or chemotherapy. Sometimes female hormones are also used to slow down the activity of the prostate.

> Of all the self-fulfilling prophecies in our culture, the assumption that ageing means decline and poor health is probably the deadliest.
>
> *Marilyn Ferguson*

DIABETES

Diabetes, a condition that makes the absorption of starch and sugar from the blood difficult, is easy to diagnose, and though there is as yet no cure it is possible to keep the disease under control with medication. As with every illness we have mentioned, it is important to go to the doctor the moment you suspect there is something wrong. And by the time we hit 50 most of us have enough experience of our own bodies to know when something is not quite right.

SYMPTOMS

Symptoms of type 1 diabetes usually arrive suddenly, whereas type 2 diabetes often develops more gradually, and symptoms may be subtle, increasing over a period of time. The symptoms, however, are basically the same, and they are related to high blood glucose levels, or hyperglycaemia. The classic symptoms of people with diabetes are:

- increased frequency of urination;
- increased thirst;
- weight loss despite increased appetite.

Sometimes hyperglycaemia can also cause:

- blurred vision;
- weakness and fatigue;
- infections, especially yeast infections.

The early symptoms of type 1 diabetes are frequently overlooked, and by the time someone realises you are unwell you may be in a state of diabetic ketoacidosis (DKA), or diabetic coma. DKA is a very serious complication, a medical emergency that requires immediate treatment. Symptoms of DKA, in addition to the symptoms of hyperglycemia, may include:

- nausea;
- vomiting;

- fatigue and lethargy;
- fruity breath odour;
- dehydration;
- hyperventilation;
- abdominal pain.

TREATMENT

The most common form of diabetes is treated by administering insulin, which has to be injected. Patients have to monitor their blood sugar levels carefully and keep to a strict diet. Older people are more likely to get type 2 diabetes (until recently it was called 'Maturity Onset' simply because sufferers tend to be older). This may be treated with pills rather than injections, but keeping to a diet will also be an important part of the treatment.

CLINICAL DEPRESSION

Depression is one of the nastiest illnesses know to man. Of the ten most common complaints for which people visit their doctor, depression comes top of the list. Although in the vast majority of cases it can be successfully treated, it is notoriously hard to diagnose and therefore many people suffer for years without help. Some become so desperate that they commit suicide.

The problem with depression is that sufferers don't realise they have an illness. They suffer feelings of anxiety, dread and despair but don't understand that the feelings they have are caused by the illness. Depressives often find themselves worrying about impending old age and death, and it seems quite natural to them to feel this way because, after all, everyone worries about these things from time to time. What they fail to understand is that whereas most people have the ability to shut out such thoughts and get on with the business of living, depressed people get quite overwhelmed by morbid introspection.

The difference between people who do not suffer from depression and those who do is a bit like the difference between car drivers and motorcyclists. Both groups hurl themselves along the motorway at high speed, but the drivers, shut up in their little metal boxes listening to some relaxing music, are hardly aware of the danger; the motorcyclists, on the other hand, are in close contact with the road and the elements and have an all too vivid picture of potential dangers.

Those who do not suffer from this illness find it hard to understand and often assume that the sufferers are simply being self-indulgent. They feel that depressives should 'count their blessings' and 'pull themselves together'. They say things like, 'We all feel a bit fed up sometimes', or 'Just think of all the people in the world with real problems!' It's not that they mean to be unkind, it's just that without having had the experience of being depressed it is impossible to know how it feels. The situation is not made any easier by the fact that depressed patients often agree that their fears are pointless and feel guilty about making such a fuss. They feel ungrateful for the good things in life and even believe that in some strange way their depression is a punishment for ingratitude.

SYMPTOMS

How do you know if you're depressed? First, depression runs in families, so if there is a history of depression in your family it is possible you will inherit it. But you don't have to come from a long line of depressives in order to be afflicted by the illness. It can be brought on by things that happen in your life. You might lose someone close to you; you might be made redundant at work; you might break up with your partner, or suffer some other sudden change in your circumstances. The list of possible causes is in fact endless. The point is that once the depression has started it takes on a life of its own. Even if your original problem is resolved, the depression won't go away. It's like Pandora's box: once opened, all the ills of the world are let loose.

Here are some of the tell-tale signs of depression:

- a persistent sadness, anxiety or 'empty' feeling;
- sleeping too little or sleeping too much;
- reduced appetite and weight loss, or increased appetite and weight gain;
- loss of interest or pleasure in activities you normally enjoy;
- restlessness and/or irritability;
- difficulty concentrating, remembering, or making decisions;

- fatigue or loss of energy;
- feeling guilty, hopeless or worthless;
- thoughts of death or suicide.

If you have some or all of these symptoms and they don't go away within a couple of weeks then it is highly likely that you are depressed.

TREATMENT

Fortunately, depression is treatable, but you will need the help of a sympathetic doctor. Although most doctors these days do understand what depression is like, there are still some who belong to the 'pull yourself together' school of thought. If you have one of these, find a new doctor. There are drugs that are effective in treating depression, and with luck one of them will suit you and your depression will be brought under control. However, once you have had depression you are more likely to suffer another episode some time in the future. This means that if you want to live a trouble-free life you need to monitor your condition carefully and seek help the moment you think another episode is on its way.

> Old age needs so little, but needs that little so much.
> *Margaret Willour*

If you are depressed, there are a couple of things you can do to help. One is to stay busy. The more you keep your mind occupied, the less time it will have to plague you with morbid thoughts. Another strategy is to take plenty of exercise. Physical exertion releases natural opiates in the brain that have a positive effect on your mood. If you make a habit of exercising several times a week you will find that your mood improves. At the moment the exercise cure is very much in vogue, to the extent that some doctors feel it should replace the use of anti-depressant drugs. This is a reaction to the over-prescribing of anti-depressants that has taken place in recent years. You might find that exercise alone conquers your depression, but, if it doesn't, then you must go back to the doctor and insist on being given a course of anti-depressants. This is not a situation where you ought to struggle on unaided, and if you need drugs to get better you must have them.

Strangely, older people are not more likely than youngsters to get depression. Common sense might tell us that the elderly have more reason to be depressed, but, for once, common sense is wrong. In fact, it is a worrying trend that increasingly children and teenagers are becoming sufferers.

Still, huge strides have been made in the treatment of this horrible illness, and with luck, one day soon medical science will find a way to kick it into the wastebin of history.

EASY WAYS TO STAY FIT

While it is true that some people live to a ripe old age without taking any special precautions, it would be foolish for us to assume that we are among the lucky few. Most of us need to work at staying fit. If you want to stay fit and healthy you need to take enough exercise to keep your body in trim. This might sound like another blinding glimpse of the obvious, but, sadly, it is not uncommon to come across people not yet in their fifties who can no longer run for a bus or climb a flight of stairs. What do they expect to be like in twenty years' time?

To stay fit takes only a moderate amount of effort, and the rewards are enormous. The problem is that for many people exercise is a bore. The prospect of spending many hours sweating in a gym while pumping iron or rowing frantically does not appeal to most of us.

> To get back my youth I would do anything in the world, except take exercise, get up early, or be respectable.
>
> *Oscar Wilde*

But it really doesn't have to be like that. Medical advice these days is that you should do at least 30 minutes' exercise five days a week. This is quite a lot to fit into a busy life, but there are some quite pleasant ways to get the exercise you need.

Before you start you need to consider what state you are in right now. If you haven't exercised much in recent years it is important to take it slowly and gently at first. Before you do anything energetic you need to go to your doctor and get your blood pressure checked. Even if you get a clean bill of health you need to proceed cautiously for two reasons. First, if you suddenly use muscles and tendons that have been inactive for years you will almost certainly strain something and end up worse off than you were before. Second, people tend to throw themselves into an exercise regime with great gusto and then, after a couple of weeks, get sick of the effort and give up. It is much better to make small changes at a comfortable pace than to try to turn your life around in one go.

WARMING UP

The first thing you need to do is some gentle bending and stretching. Even if you decide to do no other exercise at all it is important to do some stretches because they will not only help you to remain supple but will improve your balance. Stretching also protects you from strains when you are doing more vigorous exercise. You should *always* start an exercise session with a series of stretches. If you don't know how to go about this there are plenty of internet sites that give instructions. Here are just a few you can look at:

- home.earthlink.net/~fitness_habit/3_Stretching.htm
- www.webhealthcentre.com/general/ft_flexi.as
- www.nia.nih.gov/exercisebook/chapter4_stretching.htm
- secure.ehealthconnection.com/fitness/approot/owl/content /stretching.asp
- www.sport-fitness-advisor.com/stretchingexercises.html

And once you are fully warmed up, what next? Exercise doesn't *have* to involve long, sweaty sessions in the gym. We can safely assume that you are not a person who enjoys working out because if you were you would not be reading this section of the book. So let's assume that you are attracted to the idea of getting enough exercise to keep you healthy without devoting all your spare time to it. There are a number of choices open to you.

WALKING

Walking is one of life's great pleasures. It combines physical exercise with mental relaxation; it gives you the chance to see interesting places and to study plants, trees and wildlife; and it can be adapted precisely to your own requirements: you can do anything from a quick stroll round the block to long-distance treks through mountainous countryside. I have to admit that I'm far from impartial when it comes to walking because it is my favourite leisure activity. When you're feeling good, a walk gives you an extra glow of satisfaction and achievement; when you're feeling down, it helps to lighten your mood.

As with any other form of exercise, you should start off gently. If you haven't walked much recently don't go mad and try something that is beyond your ability. If you do you probably won't suffer much more than some aching muscles and painful blisters, but that might be enough to put you off walking altogether. So start off with a short walk, and wear comfortable shoes. But for the walk to have any health benefits you need to move at a brisk pace. This doesn't mean that you have to go in for what is called 'power walking'. Just pick a comfortable pace that requires you to make a little physical effort to keep it up.

Michael Foot

Many years ago I happened to be walking through London's Leicester Square when I noticed a couple of American tourists looking lost. Just then, an elderly gentleman came along walking at a brisk pace. The Americans stopped him and asked whether he knew the way to the Houses of Parliament. He told them that he did and gave them instructions on how to get there. He added that he was going that way as well but couldn't take time to guide them because he had some appointments to keep and was in a hurry, but if they kept him in sight they would be certain to find their way. Then he set off again, swinging his walking stick as he made his way energetically through the crowded streets. The Americans set off in pursuit, and it was clear that they would have to hurry if they were to stand any chance of keeping him in sight. I overheard them saying what a 'nice old guy' he had been. They were obviously quite unaware that their guide was Michael Foot, the leader of the Labour Party, then in his late sixties. Now, having just entered his nineties, he is still full of mental vigour.

CLOTHING AND EQUIPMENT

Some people take great delight in buying expensive hiking gear, but unless you intend to walk in bad weather or to cover inhospitable ground you don't really need to wear anything special. However, in summer you should remember that you might have to force your way through high grass, undergrowth or beds of nettles. Wearing shorts, therefore, might not be a great idea. And in winter you should take more precautions. You need clothing that is warm and waterproof, and a woolly hat is a good idea. You also need boots that are waterproof, and you should make sure that you wear thick socks to keep your feet warm. There are few things that put you off walking quite as much as having cold feet.

One of the best ways of getting around is to go to your local book-shop and buy a book of walks that covers the area you are inter-ested in. The people who write them have actually walked the routes they describe and can give you detailed first-hand infor-mation. The other advantage is that these walks are always way-marked with signs telling you which way to go. Even so, you need to follow the instructions very carefully. Don't try to make the description in the book fit with the bit of countryside you happen to be in. It can be tempting – and I speak from painful experience – but you will end up getting lost. Fortunately, any walk in Britain is never too far from civilisation, so even if you do get a bit lost you will eventually be able to make your way back to base.

If you decide to walk in open countryside, you'll need a map and compass. It's also important to tell someone where you're going and leave with them a copy of your itinerary (see 'Getting lost' on page 96). Make sure that you take warm clothing and something to eat and drink. A mobile phone is a good idea too. These days serious walkers often take a strong but lightweight stick with them; some people even walk with two sticks, which seems a tad excessive. The sticks help you over tricky ground and also allow you to transfer some of your weight so that your legs and feet don't have to put up with the whole burden. You don't have to be self-conscious about using a stick because even young, fit walk-ers have them.

RAMBLERS ASSOCIATION

If you enjoy walking with others, you might like to join the Ramblers Association. They also campaign about countryside issues, help to protect rights of way which might otherwise fall into disuse, and are a good source of information about the countryside code and other matters.

- Ramblers Association Main Office, 2nd Floor Camelford House, 87–90 Albert Embankment, London SE1 7TW (tel: 020 7339 8500; fax: 020 7339 8501; website www.ramblers.org.uk).
- Ramblers Association Scotland, Kingfisher House, Auld Mart Business Park, Milnathort, Kinross KY13 9DA (tel: 01577 861222; fax: 01577 861333; website: www.ramblers.org.uk/scotland).
- Ramblers Association Wales, 1 Cathedral Road, Cardiff CF11 9HA (tel: 029 2034 3535; website: www.ramblers.org.uk/wales).

> We grow old more through indolence than through age.
> *Queen Christina of Sweden*

SWIMMING

The great thing about swimming is that it gently exercises the whole body. Because of the resistance of the water it is just about impossible to make jerky movements which might result in injury, making it an ideal form of exercise for older people. There is also something very relaxing about being in water, and a regular swimming session will not only strengthen your whole body, it will also put you in a good mood for the rest of the day.

Public swimming pools are usually arranged so that people of different levels of ability are kept together. If you're a beginner, you don't really want to be sharing space with people who rush past doing a fast front crawl. If you have never learnt to swim – and a surprising number of adults haven't – you needn't be discouraged: most pools organise lessons for adult learners. The teachers are usually friendly and encouraging, and there is often a sense of camaraderie among members of the group. It won't be long before they have you swimming with great confidence.

Subscriptions to local swimming pools are quite cheap. If you want to avoid competing for space with hordes of kids, you can splash out on membership of a private club.

CYCLING

There are several advantages to cycling that make it an attractive way to get your exercise:

- It requires less physical effort than walking but allows you to cover much greater distances in less time.
- It sets you free to explore wherever you want, combining exercise with touring attractive countryside.
- You can carry quite a lot of equipment on a bike, so you can combine your cycling with other activities, such as painting, photography or camping.
- You can cycle alone or with friends, or you can join a club and cycle with a group of fellow enthusiasts.

You can spend as little or as much on your bike as you want: you can pick up an old boneshaker for next to nothing or part with a vast sum for the sleekest of racing machines or the sturdiest of mountain bikes. The two things you really do need are a comfortable saddle and some gears. You don't really want to sit on one of those razor-sharp racing saddles at your age, do you? Nor do you want to puff and pant up slopes in a high gear.

Inhaling exhaust fumes as you ride is not a very pleasant experience, and even worse is the way some motorists drive, with a reckless disregard for the safety of cyclists. So on the whole it's more fun to stick to country routes that don't have much traffic. You can always buy a cycle carrier for your car and take the bike to some picturesque bit of countryside where you can ride to your heart's content.

Of course, bicycles, like all machines, can go wrong. Tyres get punctured, gears slip, brakes fail and chains come off. So to cycle with confidence you do need to understand the workings of your bike, and to carry with you the tools and spares you may need to make repairs. In spite of this, cycling remains a very popular activity with older people.

> Though it sounds absurd, it is true to say I felt younger at 60 than I felt at 20.
>
> *Ellen Glasgow*

AEROBICS

This form of exercise has become so popular that it hardly needs an introduction. There are so many types of exercise that come under the heading 'aerobics' that it is difficult to come up with one definition, but, generally, any vigorous exercise performed to music has the 'aerobics' label stuck on it. Often the dancing exercises are supplemented by floorwork, for which you lie on a mat.

All aerobic classes require you to expend a lot of energy, and by the time you finish you will be hot, sweaty and tired. Again, it's important to break yourself in gently. Dancing energetically for an hour is not something to undertake unless your body is really up to it.

Aerobics classes are largely a female preserve, though you do come across the occasional man brave enough to exercise with the ladies. There is often a strong social element to the classes too, and people tend to go along with friends to give them moral support. You can find such classes everywhere, and with a bit of research you should be able to find one that is just right for you. They are usually inexpensive, and the only equipment you might need is an exercise mat. So, if you're feeling energetic, this could be just the sort of exercise you need.

T'AI CHI

This exercise, a form of callisthenics, originated in China. Although it has much in common with the martial arts there are important differences that make it ideal as an exercise for older people. First, t'ai chi is practised very slowly and gently. There is no leaping about, no vicious kicks and no killer blows to be delivered. Behind the slow, graceful movements there is a system of exercise that makes considerable mental and physical demands on its practitioners, but one of the good things about t'ai chi is that it is very hard to strain yourself while doing it, and over a period of time it will strengthen your body and bring peace to your mind. It will also give you an enhanced sense of balance that will serve you well in all areas of your life. In China it is widely practised by many older people who value the way it preserves their mental and physical condition as they age.

Now, t'ai chi is not easy to learn. A complete set of the short form takes about twenty minutes to complete, and to learn all the movements until you can perform the whole set without error takes quite a lot of study. You must be prepared to attend classes for several months before you are able to do it right. Even when you have the basics, the learning process doesn't end; in a sense, you will spend the rest of your life learning t'ai chi. It will reward your efforts, but if you are the sort of person who wants quick results then t'ai chi is not for you.

And to learn it well, you must have an instructor who teaches you personally. There are hundreds of books and videos on the subject, but none matches the experience of working with an instructor. The movements of t'ai chi are very precise and the only way to get them absolutely right is to have someone watch you and correct your mistakes – and tiny differences are important. At one time there just weren't any instructors except in places that had a Chinese population. Nowadays, however, t'ai chi is so popular that you can find instructors all over the place, and the courses are usually inexpensive.

If you think t'ai chi is for you, give it a try. Not only is it excellent exercise, but many people find that it becomes an absorbing hobby. Try your local library, gym or health centre for details about where evening classes are normally held in your area, and get a copy of their prospectus.

YOGA

Since yoga arrived in the West from its home in India it has become ever more popular. People like the idea of a form of exercise that is quiet and meditative. There is no sweating and straining in yoga.

Like t'ai chi, however, it is not as restful as it looks. When you start you'll be surprised at just how stiff your muscles and tendons really are. Even the simplest positions will prove to be a challenge. But if you continue to practise regularly you'll find that you do become suppler, and in time you will be able to master the more complex positions.

Again, you do need a qualified instructor to teach you. There is no shortage of books and videos on the shelves, but when you are putting your body through a series of exercises along with breathing and meditative techniques you do need an expert to ensure that you don't do yourself any harm. Fortunately, there is no shortage of yoga teachers. You will almost certainly be able to track one down giving classes somewhere in your area.

Some people do give up because they find it boring, and others are put off when they find that their body is quite unwilling to be twisted into the required positions. But if you are prepared to persevere, yoga will calm your mind while strengthening and energising your body.

> Old age is the verdict of life.
>
> *Amelia E. Barr*

THE GYM

If none of the above appeals, maybe you would like to try a workout at a gym. The advantages are that you will always find qualified staff who can advise you on the best way to exercise, and in some cases will offer you personal targets to attain so that your fitness level keeps on improving. You will be able to use a wide variety of equipment such as rowing machines, running treadmills, cycling machines and weights.

But beware – many gyms are expensive to join and many people, after paying out a hefty membership fee, give up after a few weeks and are never seen again. If you want to train at a gym, you really need to *enjoy* vigorous exercise.

AROUND THE HOUSE

There are all sorts of everyday activities that, while not performed specifically as exercise, do help you to keep fit. In the garden, for instance, by the time you've cut the lawn and dug over your vegetable patch you'll have probably had all the exercise you need for the day. Other activities such as decorating and chopping wood also count as calorie-burners and muscle-toners.

There are other everyday things you can do to increase your fitness painlessly. When you go to a shopping centre, take the stairs rather than the escalator. Take time to walk around the shops in town rather than jump in the car and drive outside town. Little things done regularly will help to improve your fitness and keep illness at bay.

READING LIST

- *Defying Age* by Dr Miriam Stoppard (Dorling Kindersley, ISBN 0751339997)
- *Yoga Over Fifty: The Way to Vitality, Health and Energy in Later Life* by Mary Stewart
- *Promoting Health in Old Age* by Miriam Bernard (Open University Press, ISBN 0335192475)
- *Alive and Kicking – The Carer's Guide to Exercises for Older People* by Julie Sobczak (Age Concern, ISBN 0862422892)
- *Better Health in Retirement* by Dr Anne Roberts (Age Concern, ISBN 0862422515)

Four

The Power of the Mind

We take the mind very much for granted, unless it stops working as we expect. This is a shame for two reasons: first, because with a bit of training your mind can accomplish many remarkable things; and second, because the mind, just like all your other faculties, needs constant maintenance to function properly.

MEMORY

We often ignore memory because for much of the time it functions without any interference from us. Memory is far more than the ability to recall where you put your car keys, it is actually who you are. It is memory that ensures that the person who wakes up in the morning is the same one who went to bed the night before. It is also memory that binds us together in families and communities by giving us a common 'story' we all remember.

> Middle age is when you've met so many people that every new person you meet reminds you of someone else.
> *Ogden Nash*

The human memory, however, is a very tricky thing. It is not in the least like the memory of a computer. If you save data on your computer, then unless there is a fault with the machine you will be able to retrieve the data at a later date and be confident that it will be 100 per cent accurate. People, on the other hand, have very quirky memories that are quite capable of forgetting information or of recalling items that have not been asked for. How many times have you forgotten an important fact, such as a PIN number, or had a sudden flash of memory in which you recall something that seems utterly irrelevant? It happens all the time.

Human memory is more than just a storage process, it is actively creative. While we get on with our daily tasks, the unconscious tinkers with memory in a variety of interesting and exasperating ways. Sometimes it throws up the answers to problems the conscious mind has been unable to find; at other times it prettifies our memory of events and makes them seem far more attractive than they actually were. Recent research has shown that the mind is also quite capable of producing vivid memories of things that never happened at all.

As we get older, the short-term memory has a tendency to let us down more often. People in middle age start to notice that a word, name or telephone number they know perfectly well will suddenly refuse to pop to the surface. If you don't do anything about it this process can continue until you start to have what some refer to as 'senior moments' – those embarrassing episodes when the car keys end up in the fridge and the marmalade gets put in the sock drawer. This is often regarded as an inevitable part of the ageing process and people accept it with as much good grace as they can muster.

> Intellectual blemishes, like facial ones, grow more prominent with age.
>
> *François de la Rochefoucauld*

It doesn't have to be that way. The memory is like a muscle: the more you use it, the stronger it gets. If you start to make a point of memorising information you will find that it gets easier, and that your memory is as sharp as it ever was. The sooner you start training your memory the more likely you are to keep it in good shape, but even those who are well into their later years can benefit from making an effort to memorise. You can use the following techniques to help you.

REPETITION

Repeating information will help you to remember it for a short while. This is fine if you want to remember, for example, a telephone number you will use only once, and quite often that is just the sort of memory we need. But if you carry on the repetition for long enough it will eventually get stored in the long-term memory. This, after all, is how we all learnt the alphabet and our times tables when we were young.

> **Test yourself**
> Below is a long number. Repeat the digits to yourself for two minutes, then carry on reading. Wait for an hour and then try to repeat the whole string. If you break the string up into smaller units, you'll find the task easier.
>
> 4389728817520

PHYSICAL REMINDERS

For reasons that are not well known, we remember things better when we associate them with other things. The most common physical reminder is to tie a knot in the corner of your handkerchief. This may seem childish, but it does work. If you plan to do something such as taking your car to be serviced, then some sort of physical reminder will prompt your memory. Another version of this technique involves leaving objects around your home in the wrong place. So when you see the sugar bowl standing on the kitchen stove it will remind you to go and cut the lawn.

> **Test yourself**
> Think of a task you have to perform later in the day. Pick something that is not part of your usual routine. Now create a physical reminder. You could tie a knot in your handkerchief, wind a rubber band around one finger, or take an object that you use frequently – the coffee jar, for example – and put it in a different place. As you arrange your reminder keep telling yourself what it is that you are supposed to remember. You'll find that this is a surefire way to make you remember the task.

ASSOCIATION

This is a curious but useful mental quirk, a sibling to the physical reminder. The more personal the association, the better it will work. For example, I needed to remember the name of Warren Street tube station. For some reason it would slip my mind. Eventually I started to think of it as Penny Lane. Why? Well, I once knew somebody called Penny Warren, and, of course, 'Penny Lane' is a well-known Beatles song. Once I'd made that association I never had any problem remembering the name.

> **Test yourself**
> Get a pack of cards and take out all the picture cards. Now choose a real person to stand for each card. For example, you might think of the King of Hearts as Jack Nicholson, the Queen of Hearts as Princess Diana, and the Jack of Hearts could be Brad Pitt. The important thing is that the association should be one that is significant to you. Now,

shuffle the cards and lay them out on a table in a grid formation. Spend some time memorising the grid, then cover it with a large sheet of paper (a newspaper would do the job adequately). See how much of the grid you can identify. Write notes, and when you have remembered as many as you can, unveil the grid and compare it with your notes. You can repeat this exercise as many times as you need until you are able to remember the entire grid.

At 20 years of age the will reigns; at 30, the wit; at 40, the judgement.

Benjamin Franklin

VISUALISATION

Some people are good at seeing mental pictures. If this applies to you, then there is a very powerful technique that can be deployed, using only the inside of your home. Let's say you have a list of things to remember; you take a mental trip around your house and place things wherever you want. For most people this technique works better if things are positioned in unlikely places. If you put bananas in the bath, for instance, you are more likely to remember than if you put them in a fruit bowl. The technique is very easy to master: I once held a seminar where one man was able to recall all but one of twenty items just a few minutes after being taught. When you get used to this technique you can change the objects you want to remember as often as you please.

Test yourself
Below is a list of twenty items you want to buy from the supermarket. Spend a few minutes looking at the list and assigning each item to a place in your house. Close your eyes and picture each item in its place. Then open your eyes, close the book, and see how many of the items you can remember. If you can remember nearly all the items, repeat the exercise tomorrow without another look at the list in the book. If you find that you cannot remember much of the list, take another look at it and repeat the exercise until you can do it successfully.

Bananas
Yoghurt
Cheese
Newspaper
Detergent
Painkillers
Wine
Flour
Pork pie
Sugar
Furniture polish
Butter
Milk
TV listings magazine
Cake
Dog food
Olive oil
Air freshener
Cauliflower
Tomatoes

MNEMONICS

If you ever learnt the colours of the spectrum by using the sentence 'Richard Of York Gives Battle In Vain', then not only do you know that the colours are red, orange, yellow, green, blue, indigo and violet, you also know what a mnemonic is. There are hundreds of common ones (for a really good collection you should look at Amanda's mnemonics page on the internet, at users.frii.com/geomanda/mnemonics.html), but the ones that work best are those you make up for yourself.

> **Test yourself**
> The planets of our solar system, starting closest to the sun and working outwards, are Mercury, Venus, Earth, Mars, Jupiter, Saturn, Uranus, Neptune and Pluto. Make up your own mnemonic using the first letter of each planet. After a couple of days, try to write out the list in the correct order. If this is too easy for you, try something a little trickier, like the last eight Olympic Games venues (Montreal, Moscow, Los Angeles, Seoul, Barcelona, Atlanta, Sydney, Athens).

> It is a man's own fault, it is from want of use, if his mind grow torpid in old age.
>
> *Samuel Johnson*

RITUAL

Something you always do in the same way becomes a memory ritual. Rituals are very useful as you get older because they highlight things that may have slipped your mind. If you can't complete a ritual to your satisfaction, you'll stop to work out which bit is missing.

Test yourself
Work out a path round your local supermarket that takes in all the sections you normally visit. Make sure that on every visit you have with you a shopping list and you follow the same path. When you feel that you have memorised the ritual, try going round the shop without referring to your shopping list. See how many items you can remember. Supermarkets used to change their displays because they thought it made them look more interesting, but then they discovered that shoppers like familiarity and hate to be confused by change, so now they only make changes occasionally.

RHYTHM AND RHYME

Can you remember your nursery rhymes? I bet you can. There is something about rhythm and rhyme that makes things easily memorable. If you take information you want to memorise and construct a rhyme around it, you'll find that it sticks in your mind with little effort.

Test yourself
Here is a list of the surnames of British prime ministers since World War Two. You can't make them rhyme, but you can make them memorable by setting the list to a melody. Take a tune you know very well and sing the names as though they were lyrics. Don't worry if the names don't

exactly fit the music because any little irregularities will make the song even more memorable. See whether you can still repeat the list a few days after you learnt it.

Attlee
Churchill
Eden
Macmillan
Douglas-Home
Wilson
Heath
Wilson
Callaghan
Thatcher
Major
Blair

If this list is too easy for you, try the prime ministers for the first half of the twentieth century (Salisbury, Campbell-Bannerman, Asquith, Lloyd George, Bonar Law, Baldwin, MacDonald, Baldwin, MacDonald, Baldwin, Chamberlain, Churchill).

> The gardener's rule applies to youth and age: when young, sow wild oats, but when old, grow sage.
>
> *H. J. Byron,* An Adage

PROCEDURAL MEMORY

Certain actions such as riding a bike or driving a car have been practised until they become automatic. This is procedural memory, and it is very useful. The interesting thing about this sort of memory is that it seems to exist in the nerves and muscles rather than the intellect. If you've ever tried to teach someone else to drive, you'll know what I mean. You can perform the actions yourself, but it's hard to describe them to someone else. What's more, when you are forced to think about what you do you can sometimes get confused and find that you make mistakes.

CONCENTRATION

People often associate an increase in age with a decrease in the ability to concentrate. There is some truth in this, but it is by no means the whole picture, nor is it an inevitable part of the ageing process. If you learn to concentrate, and practise, now you will retain that ability in years to come. Mostly it's a matter of teaching yourself a good mental habit. Unfortunately, concentration is not something we are taught at school, nor is it something we are able to do well instinctively. To concentrate effectively you need to recognise it as a skill to be acquired, and to remember to practise it regularly.

The simplest form of concentration is no more than common sense. Just pick a task and make a mental resolution to stick at it uninterrupted until it is complete. The following tips will help.

- When starting any task you need to assess how long you think it will take.
- Make sure that you have that amount of time available and try to avoid things that will interrupt you (for example, you might want to switch your telephone to voicemail).
- Make sure that as far as possible you have everything you need to complete the task. Having to stop to find the right tool – a reference book, or a piece of equipment – is a nuisance and can even lead to you being so distracted that you give up all together and turn your attention to something else.
- If the task is going to take a long time you need to break it up into smaller sections. Doing too much at once will lead to failure and disappointment.
- Reward yourself when you finish each section by giving yourself a break. You could have a cup of coffee, or take a stroll round the garden.

- When you start a section make sure you don't quit until you finish it. Even if you come across difficulties it is essential to keep going until you finish that section.
- You might find that your time estimate was wrong. You can reassess the situation, but you shouldn't make that an excuse to stop.
- When the task is finished, don't just go off and do something else. Take a little time to check what you have done to make sure it is properly finished.

It also pays to make a point of remaining mindful of what we are doing. It is very easy to put your mind on autopilot while performing routine tasks, but if you do you run the risk of forgetting what you were about. We have all had the experience of going into a room to fetch something and coming back having forgotten what it is we wanted. This is not a sign of approaching senility – the truth, contrary to popular thought, is that only a tiny minority of older people are seriously affected by senility – it's just sloppy thinking that we can make a point of avoiding.

> It is not by muscle, speed or physical dexterity that great things are achieved, but by reflection, force of character and judgement; in these qualities old age is usually not only not poorer, but is even richer.
>
> *Marcus Tullius Cicero*

If you really want to boost your powers of concentration, the following exercise will help.

- You need a small object on which to focus your concentration. Almost anything will do, but you should start with something quite simple – a box of matches, for example, or a tube of toothpaste.
- Sit in an upright chair and examine your object carefully for a couple of minutes. Try to remember every tiny detail.
- When you feel confident that you have the object fixed in your mind's eye, close your eyes and see how long you can hold that mental image in sharp focus. You'll be surprised how quickly the image fades.
- Repeat the exercise regularly until you can hold an image faultlessly for several minutes.

Nelson Mandela
There can be few stories more inspiring than that of Nelson Mandela. He was born in 1918, and after studying law he helped found the ANC, in 1944. This was the start of a long career as a political activist and campaigner against the evils of apartheid. Mandela also became involved in the armed struggle against the white regime. In 1962 he received a five-year prison sentence, but while in custody he was charged with sabotage and sentenced to life imprisonment. Though imprisonment severely curtailed his activities, he never gave up the struggle. Many men would have been broken by the harsh conditions of a South African jail, but Mandela was determined to survive. Eventually it became clear to all but the most obdurate Afrikaners that the apartheid regime had had its day. In 1990, Mandela was released and was greeted as a hero not only by his own countrymen but by those throughout the world who had opposed apartheid. By this time Mandela was in his seventies and could have been forgiven for wanting a quiet life. Instead, when free elections were held in 1994, he became president of South Africa and served in that capacity until 1999. What was extraordinary about his term in office was that he resisted all temptation to punish the whites for the evils that had been inflicted upon his countrymen. Instead he pressed for a policy of reconciliation that would allow South Africa to make a peaceful transition to full democracy. After he retired he continued to travel the world as a representative of the new South African state. Now well into his eighties, he has cut down on his commitments a little but still leads an active and purposeful life.

RELAXATION

For most of us, relaxing amounts to putting our feet up in front of the telly. But, pleasant though that can be, it doesn't amount to real relaxation. When you worry over everyday problems your body reacts by storing up tension in muscles without you even realising it. You frown, or get aches and pains in various parts of the body, and may be quite unaware that this discomfort is actually the result of tension. What's more, the tension pains will make you feel miserable and this can lower your mood even further so that you get into a vicious circle of worry and muscular pain. The tension can also affect internal organs, especially the stomach, which is very prone to muscular spasms when you get worried. In the short term, this process makes you unhappy and spoils your ability to concentrate; in the long term it may have serious effects on your health.

The answer is to eliminate the tension completely. Try to find twenty minutes every day to go through the following ritual, which will relax every group of muscles in your body. And remember, this has to be done regularly to be effective.

- Lie on the floor or on the bed, whichever you prefer. Use a pillow to support your head.
- The room should be warm, but make sure there is also fresh air.
- Now close your eyes and concentrate your attention on your breathing.
- Breath slowly and regularly from the diaphragm. As you breathe in, your stomach should go out; as you exhale, it should come in again.
- Scrunch your toes up hard and keep them that way for a slow count of five. Feel the tension in your toes. Now relax. Repeat this.

- Now point your toes downwards so that the other muscles in your feet become tense. Again, count to five and relax. Repeat.
- Now work on your calves. Pushing down with your heels will create tension in the calf muscles. Hold this for a count of five and relax. Repeat.
- Next you should tense the muscles in your thighs. Once again, keep the tension up while you count slowly to five, then relax. Repeat.
- Now tense up the muscles in your behind. Count to five, then relax. Repeat.
- Next, pull your stomach in as far as you can. Try to touch your backbone with your tummy button! Count five, then relax. Repeat.
- Now breathe in deeply and inflate your chest as far as possible. Hold your breath for a count of five, then breathe out. Repeat.
- Now clench your fists really hard while you count to five. Relax and repeat.
- Push down with the heels of your palms to tense the muscles in your forearms. Hold for a count of five, then relax. Repeat.
- Now work on the muscles in your face and head. Scrunch your face up as if you were trying to squeeze all your features into your nose. Hold for a few seconds, then do a silent scream in which you open your mouth and eyes as wide as possible. Repeat.
- You should now find that your whole body is comfortably relaxed. Just lie there and enjoy this sensation for as long as you want. If you want, you can drop off into a pleasant little nap. You will wake up feeling totally refreshed.

You may think that this is a tiresome performance to go through simply in order to relax. But if you persist with this ritual for a few weeks, you'll eventually get used to the feel of your muscles and will find that you can zoom in on areas that need relaxing without going through the entire process every time. You will also find that during your normal daily activities your muscles will tend to stay relaxed, and on the occasions when you do get stressed, you will notice which muscles are causing the problem and be better able to deal with it.

> Tranquillity is the old man's milk.
>
> *Thomas Jefferson*

VISUALISATION

This technique is very effective when used in conjunction with the deep relaxation method. The simplest sort of visualisation can be used to lift your mood.

Once you have relaxed completely, imagine yourself lying in a garden in mid-summer. Unlike a real garden, your imaginary one has no bugs, no neighbours using the lawnmower, and nothing else to disturb you. How elaborate your visualisation becomes depends on how powerful your visual imagination is. If you find visualising difficult, the best thing to do is to start with some simple details and add to them bit by bit. For example, imagine that you are lying under a shady tree with dappled sunlight falling on you. Now you can add an occasional butterfly flitting to and fro. Next you can include some flowers for the butterflies to drink from. If you build up your visualisation step by step like this you will soon have a powerful tool for enhancing your mood whenever you feel the need of it.

Of course, you don't have to stick to sunny afternoons and gardens. The great thing about imagination is that you can use whatever you want. I know someone who likes to float over Antarctica, and another person who regularly journeys through outer space naked. Furthermore, if music helps you to relax, have a CD or cassette player standing by to play whatever fits in with your mood. These days you can get recordings of all sorts of natural sounds, everything from tropical storms to the howling of wolves.

This sort of visualising is great fun, but there is a more serious use to which the technique can be put. Why not use it to help you with practical problems? If you have a difficult task to perform or you're facing a potentially awkward conversation with someone, why not visualise the whole thing in advance? For example, if you're going to do a bit of DIY, visualise the tools and materials you need and go through the whole operation step by step in your mind, paying special attention to any tricky bits and working out in advance how you are going to tackle them.

MEDITATION

If you think that meditation is just a load of New Age nonsense, maybe I could persuade you to reconsider. Unfortunately, meditation reached the West accompanied by chanting, bells, incense and all the trappings of hippy culture. That was great for people who enjoyed that sort of thing and had an interest in Eastern religions, but it tended to put off those of a more down-to-earth turn of mind, and that was a great pity because meditation is really a very practical and useful technique.

To practise it is quite easy. It certainly doesn't require you to become involved in exotic religious beliefs. It is available to just about anyone, and once you reach a certain level of ability you can do it anywhere and at any time.

Millions of people meditate because it induces feelings of serenity and well-being. When we meditate, the pattern of waves produced by the brain is altered. Our brains produce brainwaves of four frequencies. The everyday waking frequency is called Beta and has a frequency range of about 15 to 38 cycles per second (cps) and upwards. The Alpha range is 8 to 14 cps. This frequency is associated with rapid eye movement (REM) sleep, hypnosis, meditation and daydreaming. The Theta range is between 4 and 7 cps and is associated with trance-like imaginative states, deep meditation, light sleep, and most aspects of creativity. The Delta range is 0.5 to 3 cps, and usually relates to deep sleep. In the lowest levels of Delta, there are no mental images and no awareness of the body. Some meditators experience a Delta meditative state – asleep yet fully conscious.

> Old age has a great sense of calm and freedom.
>
> *Plato*

Medical research has suggested that there are numerous health benefits to be gained from regular meditation. Sometimes these claims seem just a tad overenthusiastic, but the following list contains the ones I have seen regularly reported or have experienced personally.

- It lowers consumption of oxygen and decreases the respiratory rate.
- It increases bloodflow and slows the heart rate.
- It increases exercise tolerance in heart patients.
- It leads to a state of mental serenity.
- It reduces high blood pressure.
- It can reduce anxiety attacks by lowering the levels of blood lactate.
- It eases muscle tension, pre-menstrual tension and headaches.
- It promotes feelings of self-confidence.
- It increases serotonin production, which influences mood and behaviour. Low levels of serotonin are associated with depression, obesity, insomnia and headaches.
- It eases suffering as a result of allergies, arthritis, etc.
- It aids post-operative healing.
- It is thought to bolster the immune system, and according to some research it increases the activity of 'natural-killer cells', which eliminate bacteria and cancer cells.

Aside from its 'Eastern' connotations, people are often put off meditating because it seems boring to sit completely still for ages with your eyes closed. People who try it often complain that 'nothing happens', and promptly give up. Let me ask you this – have you ever tried to learn a foreign language? If so, did you speak it fluently after the first lesson? Of course not; and meditation, just like any other skill, has to be learnt. What's more, meditation is not like other skills we acquire. We are used to acquiring knowledge a bit at a time, steadily adding to our store until we become expert at some subject or skill. Meditation doesn't work that way. It is more like a process of *un*learning, by getting rid of all the rubbish and letting your mind free itself.

Think of your mind as a muddy pond. How would you clear the water? If you thrash around, all you'll do is stir up more mud and make matters worse; but if you let the water become still, the sediment will settle to the bottom and the water will become clear.

In the West, because we have no tradition of meditation, we tend not to realise that the term covers a wide variety of techniques that are quite different and have different purposes. Let's look first at a very simple basic meditation that absolutely anyone can do. As a beginner, you'll need peace and quiet in order to practise, though eventually you should be able to meditate anywhere.

- Choose a room that is light, airy and comfortable. Don't bother sitting on the floor with your legs crossed. You haven't been brought up to sit that way, and not only will you find it painful, it is bad for your circulation. You can sit on a straight-backed chair or even on the end of your bed if you want. Sit upright and don't lean on anything.
- Imagine you have a thread with one end attached to the top of your head and the other fixed to the ceiling above you. Don't strain to be upright, just find a nice comfortable posture that allows you to stay alert. Clasp your hands lightly and let them rest in your lap.
- Now close your eyes and take a while to let your breathing become regular. As you inhale, try very gently to draw the air as far down into your tummy as possible. Try to draw the air right down until it reaches a spot just below the navel. Yes, I know that's actually impossible, but with a little practice it will *feel* possible. The Japanese call this spot the *hara* and regard it as a very important energy centre.
- Once you are happy with your breathing you should start to count your breaths. Don't count the in-breaths, but count each out-breath. When you get to ten, start again. You may think this sounds easy, but you'll soon find that a thousand thoughts will arise to put you off your counting. You'll also be more than usually aware of noises coming from outside the room. Oh, and you'll start to itch as well. This is all completely normal. Some teachers of meditation recommend facing these problems with an iron resolve and sitting impassively through whatever torments your body throws at you; I say, 'If it itches, scratch it!' Eventually you'll reach a stage where you can ignore distractions, but you don't have to be Superman from day one.

- Continue gently to bring your mind back again and again to your counting. Keep your mind on your breathing and try not to lose count. When you fail, don't blame yourself. Just have another go, and another and another. If you practise for, say, twenty minutes a day, you will find that you start not only to enjoy your meditation but to feel real benefits from it. After a while, you'll find that you look forward to each session and would be disappointed to miss one.

> He who is of calm and happy nature will hardly feel the pressure of age, but to him who is of an opposite disposition youth and age are equally a burden.
>
> *Plato*

There is another form of meditation that you might like to try. Start in the same way as before, but after you have counted your breaths for ten minutes or so, stop and just sit there, watching the contents of your mind. Do not make any effort to think of anything in particular, just watch the thoughts as they arise and pass away. You'll soon notice that your thoughts, which can sometimes seem so persistent (particularly when they are of the worrying variety), are actually flickering and insubstantial. Even the most powerful ideas are not able to sustain themselves for very long and will soon give way to other thoughts. If you are anxious or fearful, you'll come to realise that those feelings do not have the strong hold on your mind that you supposed. They actually flutter through the mind like butterflies, and if you stare at them steadfastly, they will eventually disappear. We invest much mental energy in worries of one sort or another. This constant fretting is counterproductive, and once we become aware of it we can work at changing our mental habits for the better.

Five

Money, Money, Money

There are few areas of life that are not affected by money, and as we grow older the subject becomes no less important. Put bluntly, the question you have to face is, 'Can I afford to grow old?'

On the one hand, pensioners should be better off. Once the mortgage has been paid off and the children are financially independent, parents should find themselves with plenty of spare cash with which to enjoy their retirement. Unfortunately, that is not the whole story. Many people who have paid regularly into pension plans have now found that they are not getting the returns they expected. Some people who are still in work are being told that their eventual pension will not be worth what they thought it would. For some years the stock market has under-performed and money invested on behalf of pensioners has not grown at the expected rate. As if this were not enough, many people find themselves saddled with endowment mortgages which, when they mature, will not provide sufficient funds to pay off the sum borrowed.

> The best thing to save for old age is yourself.
>
> *Anon.*

We talked in Part Two about people who want to carry on working after they have officially retired (see 'Work' on page 62). It now seems that many of us will not have a choice in the matter as we have been warned by politicians that we can now expect to work to the age of 70. This is a matter of grave concern to many older people, not simply because they don't want to continue working but because they are not at all sure there will be the jobs available. How will the economy cope with thousands of extra people all seeking jobs? Unsurprisingly, this is not a matter to which politicians seem to have given much thought.

People in later life often expect to inherit money from their parents. If, however, the parents are forced through ill health to go into a care home, then much or all of your inheritance may be swallowed up in fees. Even worse, when all the money from the sale of your parents' house is gone, they are entitled to be looked after by the state. But the level of care provided is not up to the standard of many private care homes, so if you wish your parents to live out their lives in relative comfort you will be asked to stump up the difference in fees between a council-run home and a private one.

PLANNING

Faced with what might become a difficult financial situation, it is necessary to do a bit of advanced planning. It is a good idea to set down your entire financial situation as it is now and as you expect it to be when you reach a notional retirement age. The good news is that your expenses should diminish. If you're lucky enough to have paid off your mortgage, then that is one major saving. If your children are no longer financially dependent on you, that will block another hole through which much of your money has leaked in the past. If you are no longer commuting long distances to work, that is another saving made. If you have been running two cars, you might now be able to make do with one. Furthermore. as a retired person you are entitled to concessions for a wide variety of services, and you should take full advantage of these. Whenever you are asked to pay any sort of fee you should enquire about concessions for OAPs. People always make jokes about the bus pass, but this and other concessions can make a big difference to your budget.

Make a list of all your assets. Include not just cash in the bank but absolutely everything you own. Add in any income you get for working, income from any other area, and any pension payments you're receiving. If you don't know what your house is worth, you need to get it valued. Call in two or three estate agents so that you have more than one opinion to guide you. A valuation should be given free of charge – and there is, of course, no obligation to go ahead with a sale.

> Time ripens all things; no man is born wise.
> *Miguel de Cervantes*

Once you have a clear idea of your wealth, you can work out whether your income is enough to support your outgoings. If it is, then you have no problems, but what if it isn't? Is it time to cut down your expenses, or even to consider selling the family silver?

FINDING ADVICE

Before you make any drastic decisions about your finances you need to get the best advice you can. Here's a list of some good sources:

- National newspapers. The Saturday edition of the *Daily Telegraph* and Wednesday's *Daily Mail* both have useful sections.
- Radio. On BBC Radio 2, for instance, you can tune in to the Jeremy Vine show from noon until 2 p.m. There, not only can you benefit from general advice given by their experts, you can also write or phone in with questions of your own.
- The Consumers' Association publishes *Money Which?*, a supplement to the main magazine that deals with a wide range of financial questions.
- Don't ignore the huge amount of free information available to elderly people from institutions such as the Inland Revenue and the Financial Services Authority, though this can overwhelm you with detail. It is best to start your search at your local Citizens Advice Bureau where you will find helpful staff who are used to dealing with the needs of the elderly and will point you in the direction of the information you need.

INDEPENDENT FINANCIAL ADVISER

You may decide you need something more than general advice, and in that case you can arrange to meet an independent financial adviser. Picking the right person for this crucial role could hardly be more important. The best way is to have someone recommended to you by a client who has had satisfactory service in the past. Since almost everyone has to seek financial advice at some point, it is worth asking around among friends, relatives and colleagues until you find one who has a really good reputation. You can simply go through the *Yellow Pages* until you find someone in your area, but this is a rather hit-or-miss approach. I've done it myself, with unhappy results.

Other than reputation, the main criterion is simple: the adviser must save you money. But there are other factors to take into account, such as whether the person is easy to get on with; whether he or she will make home visits out of hours; and whether he or she explains your options in language you can understand. Good financial advisers are quite thin on the ground, so, as always, do your research.

Hokkusai

The celebrated Japanese artist Hokkusai was regarded as a highly accomplished painter throughout his adult life. His own judgement was far more severe. He thought that everything he had done before 50 was rubbish; it was only when he turned 70 that he felt he was producing work of real quality. And as he lay on his deathbed in his late eighties he mourned the fact that his artistic development was not complete. 'If only heaven had granted me five more years,' he remarked with a sigh, 'I would have become a real painter.'

REDUCING YOUR DEBTS

You don't really want to start cutting down on expenditure at this stage. After all, you have worked long and hard for this retirement and you didn't go through all that so that you could live at subsistence level in your old age. But if you owe money on credit cards, store cards, hire purchase agreements or other forms of lending, this is the time to get rid of those debts if you can. Borrowed money is always expensive, and using credit cards to borrow money is just crazy. It may be hard to pay off all your debts, but if you are able to do it you will immediately begin to save money.

> A man must have grown old and lived long in order to see how short life is.
>
> *Arthur Schopenhauer*

There are many companies who offer to buy up your debts and consolidate them into one loan, with repayments less than they used to be. This sounds very appealing, and the TV ads always show satisfied customers sighing with relief, but you need to approach offers of this sort with great caution. One thing you can be certain of is that these people are not loaning money out of kindness. Read the small print with great care, and, if possible, get independent advice before you decide to go ahead. You may well find that though you pay less in interest, the period of the loan is much extended and you will be paying it off for years to come. And, of course, the whole time you are paying interest.

CUTTING BACK

If after doing this you still can't find enough money to support your lifestyle then it is time to look at your budget and see where savings can be made. This is very much a last resort. There is no shortage of stories of pensioners living on a fixed income who endure a miserable and frugal existence trying to survive on inadequate funds. This is not the way any of us would choose to live out our days, but sadly, some people will find themselves in this condition.

You could make a start by seeing if you can make savings on any monthly premiums you pay. There are many insurance companies, for instance, willing to offer special deals to older customers. You can trawl through the ads on TV and in newspapers and magazines, and you can run searches on the internet, but another very good source of information is Age Concern. You can write to them at Age Concern England, Astral House, 1268 London Road, London SW16 4ER (tel: 020 8765 7200; website: www.ageconcern.org.uk).

If you are in real need, there are numerous charities that are willing to help. Did the institution you worked for have a benevolent fund to help former employees? Many do, and it is worth finding out if you are entitled to claim. You should also consult Charity Choice, either by finding their directory in your local library or searching their website at www.charitychoice.co.uk. This site lists hundreds of charities and you may well find one that can aid you. For example, as an author I could apply to the Society of Authors for financial help should I fall on hard times.

STARTING YOUR OWN BUSINESS

Having had a look at your outgoings, what about finding ways to raise extra money? Some sort of part-time work would help (see 'Work' on page 62), or perhaps you could start up a little business of your own. Plenty of retired people who spent years in salaried employment have found when they retired that they actually have the talent to run their own business. For example, I came across a man who'd spent his whole career in the accounts department of a giant motor corporation and had stuck it out because it seemed a safe job. When he retired he had the idea of buying up caravans, refurbishing them and selling them on. Within a year he had a flourishing business that brought in far more than he'd ever made as an accountant.

How do you get started in business? First you need to find a gap in the market. What goods or services are needed in your area? Is there anything that is needed but hard to find? If you think your business will be confined to your immediate locality, then you might talk to friends and neighbours and canvass opinions. What sort of business do they think is lacking in your area? Alternatively, you may be thinking of a business that has a much wider appeal, with customers all over Britain and perhaps abroad as well. For example, an acquaintance of mine was on holiday in Spain when he came across some beautiful hand-made ceramic tiles. He bought some for himself and arranged with the company to ship them back to the UK. Once he'd fitted them in his home, visitors always admired them and wanted to know where they were from. He now has a thriving business importing ceramic tiles.

> I am long on ideas, but short on time. I expect to live to be only about 100.
>
> *Thomas Edison*

If you don't have any business experience, you can get advice from your bank. Most banks these days provide a service helping new businesses to get started. It is worth their taking a little trouble over small businesses because they hope to do your banking if you become successful. Compare offers from several banks to make sure you are getting the best advice and most favourable terms. Also, you will need to register with the Inland Revenue, which publishes a wide range of leaflets advising those who wish to work for themselves on the legal requirements.

CASHING IN ON EQUITY

Don't forget that if you own a house you have a very valuable asset and it is possible to free up some of the cash that you have invested in your home. There are various ways to do this.

The most drastic is to sell the house and buy something cheaper. You may feel that now the children are off your hands you could manage in smaller accommodation. Older people often look for bungalows, flats, or even large caravans as a solution to their accommodation problem. First, however, you must be sure that the new home isn't too small. There are few things more likely to cause domestic rows than being shut up in a confined space together. Second, you won't be the only elderly couple who've had this idea. Where you find accommodation of this sort you will also find that most of the occupants are elderly. This is fine if you are the sort of person who enjoys being with a lot of people your own age, but not so good if you want to live in a more diverse sort of community.

> Youth is the gift of nature, but age is a work of art.
> *Stanislaw J. Lec*

Alternatively, you could keep the house but remortgage it. This will also provide you with a lump sum, and it may be very useful, but will it be enough to last you for the rest of your life? Also, the value of the property you leave to your children will decrease substantially and you may feel that you don't want to profit at their expense. There is no shortage of companies willing to offer you a remortgage, and several of them can be found just by watching the ads on TV. A flick through the *Yellow Pages* or a quick browse on the internet will bring up many more. Consider the offers they make, but also consider the long-term implications. After spending years paying off your mortgage, do you really want to mortgage the property again?

STATE BENEFITS

It is important to discover exactly how much state aid you are entitled to. The principal benefit for older people is the state pension. During winter, the government also authorises cold-weather payments where necessary. If you are 75 or over you are also entitled to a free TV licence. However, there are numerous other benefits for which you might be eligible.

A cynic may think that the government is not too keen on older citizens being made aware of all their entitlements because it would be expensive if everyone made claims, but that's not so. The governing rules are complicated, however. A visit to your local Citizens Advice Bureau will help to clarify exactly how much help you are entitled to, but your best way of finding out is to approach the Department for Work and Pensions (Room 539, The Adelphi, 1–11 John Adam Street, London WC2N 6HT; website: www.dwp.gov.uk).

Some people feel bad about seeking state aid because they think it is like taking charity. This is simply not so. You, and probably your partner, have been paying taxes all your lives and any help you now get from the state is no more than you deserve, so it is sensible to take every penny you are owed.

And don't forget to take advantage of any OAP concession!

LIVING ABROAD

Finally, it's worth reiterating that another way to reduce your expenditure is to live abroad in a place where the cost of living is lower (see 'Where to Live?' on page 48). This can sound attractive, and for some people it is the answer, but there are a number of financial matters to be taken into account. First, you need to make sure that the country you are going to really will be cheaper than the UK. If you have only been there on holiday you will know the cost of food, drink and entertainment, but what about other costs such as utilities, local taxes and medical services?

This information can be difficult to come by while you are in the UK so it might be an idea to go on a fact-finding tour and get answers to all the questions you need to ask. You could consult the Tourist Information Office local to where you intend to buy, and local estate agents. It would also be worth looking for other ex-pats and asking for their advice. They will probably be only too happy to give you a helping hand. If you ask around, there is probably a bar or club somewhere that they use as a meeting place.

> Old age is not so bad when you consider the alternatives.
> *Maurice Chevalier*

And don't neglect your situation in the UK. Will you still be entitled to your state pension? If so, will it keep rising or will it remain fixed at the level it was when you left the country? Are you going to be liable to pay tax in the UK? The rules for tax and pensions are complicated, and much depends on where you are going – you will probably, for example, do better if you are moving to an EU country. The Inland Revenue and the Department for Work and Pensions will be happy to provide you with the information you need; you can find them either in the telephone directory or via the internet.

Six

Family Affairs

If you are making plans for your retirement, it is likely that you are between 50 and 60 and that your children are anywhere between secondary school age and their mid-thirties. This raises a number of issues that also need careful consideration.

REBELLIOUS TEENS

Just as some children reach puberty later than others, so some adolescents are not necessarily ready to be adults by the age of eighteen. This is a major change in the lives of both the children and their parents. How you handle this difficult period will have a strong influence on the sort of relationship you will have with your children in later life.

The rapid hormonal changes that take place in teenagers are notorious for causing wild mood swings. This is as alarming for the teenager as it is for the parents. Suddenly a previously happy child is transformed into a surly, moody, aggressive brat who seems to take delight in opposing the parents at every turn. The resulting friction is frequently distressing to all parties involved. The parents feel they have done the best they can for their off-spring and don't deserve the rough treatment being handed out to them; the teenager is being pulled in two directions at once: there is a desire to be independent – the 'I'm not a kid any more!' syndrome – but there is also a lot of fear and confusion because for the first time there is the prospect of facing life without parental protection. As if that were not enough, the adolescent body is changing rapidly. Hair starts to grow in places it never grew before, while breasts, menstruation and acne all make an appearance. It's not surprising that the average teenager is moody and confused.

> When you are younger you get blamed for crimes you never committed, and when you're older you begin to get credit for virtues you never possessed. It evens itself out.
>
> *Casey Stengel*

It is hard when you are being roundly abused by your teenage kids to hold on to the thought that it is just a mood swing that will pass as quickly as it arrived. Some teenagers have an absolute genius for finding the most hurtful thing to say. Also, they can be very good at being lazy, untidy, unhelpful and self-centred. No matter what you do at this juncture it will be wrong, because as far as your teenager is concerned being wrong is your purpose in life. If you talk to their friends, they say, 'Why do you always embarrass me in front of my friends?' If you don't, they say, 'Why do you hate everybody I bring home?'

What can you do?

COPING STRATEGIES

The one thing you really shouldn't do is take everything they say and do at face value and act as if they really mean it. If you join them in shouting, banging doors and hurling insults, you are not only playing a losing game – because they do all those things so much better than you – you are also losing their respect. Keeping calm is very hard, but in the end it is a winning strategy, even though a measured, reasonable reply to a torrent of adolescent abuse usually gets the response, 'You are *so patronising*!' Staying calm doesn't mean that you have to put up with everything that's thrown at you, of course, or that you can never criticise your off-spring's behaviour, but comfort yourself with the thought that teenagers *do* notice your attempts to lower the temperature and will, eventually, be grateful to you.

> In bringing up a child, think of its old age.
> *Joseph Joubert*

Most teenagers are not in full-on rebellion mode all the time, so another constructive thing to do is to use the lull between the storms to do things together and chat pleasantly about things that interest you both. There's no reason why you shouldn't be able to empathise with a number of things your kids are con-cerned about, and you can certainly discuss them in a way your parents probably never could. Try to understand their music, try to take an interest in their fashions (but don't go so far as to wear them yourself!); you can also share their enthusiasm for the internet and all the wonders of our hi-tech world. On that basis you can also talk to them about sensitive subjects such as drugs and sex without resorting to the sort of hysterical, ill-informed ranting that was so depressingly prevalent in our parents' generation.

YOUR OFFSPRING'S FRIENDS

Despite your efforts, teenagers, and especially girls, are often deeply involved with their friends and regard them as the only people in the world who understand them and with whom they can talk freely. Parents who criticise those friends are living dangerously. You run the risk of alienating your offspring, who will immediately seek solace with the very people you object to. So before you say anything at all on the subject you need to think carefully about what you are going to say and why you are saying it.

Are the friends really a bad influence on your child? This is the most common parental complaint. But before you make it, think carefully about whether it is true. If you think your child is being led into smoking, drug taking, truancy, vandalism or under-age sex, then of course you need to do something about it. But if all the friends are doing is dressing strangely, lazing around and generally behaving like teenagers, you need to keep quiet. At this age kids change so rapidly that it is hard to keep up with who their friends are. This week's best friend can easily become next week's reject. Similarly, the things kids like to do change overnight. So if you object to them hanging around on a street corner chatting to a bunch of people wearing strange clothes, you need to remember that in a month's time they might have given that up and found something new to do with their time.

DATING

When your child first has a boyfriend or girlfriend, all the above warnings seem to be highlighted. Criticise the love of your child's life at your peril! To you they may seem like a couple of silly kids who have a crush on each other, but in their hearts and minds they are Romeo and Juliet. Before you interfere, you need to be very sure that what you are doing is really necessary.

> Youth would be an ideal state if it came a little later in life.
> *Herbert Asquith*

Contrary to popular belief, most teenagers are quite sensible. They often have a quite well-developed moral sense of their own and don't need to be lectured constantly about the right way to behave. If you do that, you will only force them to assert their independence by doing the opposite of what you want.

I was once one of the moderators on a teenagers' email list, in the days before instant messaging. The kids would post emails that were then copied to all members of the list. It was the job of the moderators to make sure that no unauthorised people got access to the list and that the members didn't do anything too dreadful. Sometimes they would use bad language and one of the other moderators decided, without consulting anyone else, to publish a notice banning all swearing from the list. What happened? For several weeks there was an outpouring of the filthiest language you have ever heard. Even kids who were normally rather quiet joined in and started swearing fluently. What had been achieved? The exact opposite of what was intended, plus the fact that the kids had less trust in the good sense of the moderators than they had before.

If your children know deep down that you are really concerned for their own good and not merely trying to assert your authority or your own preferences, then you stand much more of a chance of having constructive dialogue with them when you feel you need to. A parent who has spent many years yelling 'Don't do that!' and 'You *must* do this!' is not likely to be listened to on the matter of suitable boyfriends and girlfriends.

YOUNG ADULTS?

Eventually your children will reach eighteen and officially be adults. This brings with it a whole set of new challenges. Just because they are old enough to vote or fight for their country does not mean that they are grown up in any real sense. There are some youngsters who are remarkably mature at that age, but they are in the minority. Although the worst of the teenage tantrums should now be over, that doesn't mean your children have turned into helpful, considerate, responsible adults. They are likely to need your help just as much as they ever did.

> In case you're worried about what's going to become of the younger generation, it's going to grow up and start worrying about the younger generation.
>
> *Roger Allen*

Being a young adult can be even scarier than being a teenager. It suddenly dawns on them that they no longer live in a world populated by parents and teachers who are all anxious to help; now they have to deal with adults from outside that cosy circle who will not make allowances for their age or may not have their best interests at heart.

Problems associated with money, relationships, study and accommodation as well as simple day-to-day things such as cooking for themselves hove into view. To be fair, girls on the whole handle such matters better than boys. Many girls are naturally quite self-reliant; they also have a useful habit of banding together in groups that offer mutual support. Boys often face their problems alone, but girls can count on all their friends to rally round with help, encouragement and advice.

HOW MUCH SHOULD YOU HELP?

The problem for parents at this stage is to know just how much they should be prepared to help. This is always a ticklish issue, because on the one hand you don't want your offspring to get into serious difficulties, but on the other you do want them to learn to be self-reliant.

There is no easy solution. It is one of those potentially awkward issues you need to confront as it arises. You need to encourage your children to cope by themselves as best they can but to feel that they can still call on parental help if the going gets too rough. It is important while they are growing up to do what you can to prepare them for the responsibilities of adulthood. Get them to do things like cook a meal for the family, where you can, if necessary, step in to help. Teenage boys can be particularly clueless and badly need to develop some life skills. This may take some time, and they will probably need quite a lot of encourage-ment, so the sooner you get started the better. You don't want them to leave home only to find that they can't boil an egg, pay a bill or run a car, for that won't do their self-confidence any good at all.

> ### Pablo Picasso
> Picasso has a reputation that spreads far beyond the confines of the art world. For many he is the personification of modern art. He was born in 1881 and died in 1973 at the age of 92. His later life is remarkable for the way in which he retained his energy and enthusiasm well into old age. On a personal level, he fathered a daughter in 1949 when he was 68 years old. On a professional level, he commemorated his 85th birthday in 1966 by holding three simultaneous exhibitions of his work in Paris. Between March and October 1964 he completed 347 etchings, mainly on erotic themes. In 1969 he painted an astonishing 140 canvasses. His 90th birthday was commemorated with an exhibition in the Grande Galerie of the Louvre; he was the first living artist to be honoured in this way. Picasso is not just an inspiration to other artists, but to all of us who would like to live with energy and purpose right through to the end of our lives.

MUTUAL RESPECT

My eldest cousin, a doctor who had just become a fellow of the Royal College of Surgeons, was home on a visit where he found his mother suffering from a painful ear ache. He took a look at the problem and then went to the local chemist's to get an ointment to treat it with. He came back and was about to apply the ointment when his mother asked, 'Did the chemist say it was all right to use this stuff?'

> For the first half of your life, people tell you what you should do; for the second half, they tell you what you should have done.
>
> *Richard Needham*

It is one of the hardest things to accept that one's children are fully qualified adults. When you have spent years changing their nappies, dressing grazed knees and wiping snotty noses, it is hard to believe that they might have perfectly sound views on the situation in the Middle East, on who is going to win the Premier League, or on exactly what has gone wrong with dad's computer.

Adults have a number of little tricks that have the effect of keeping kids under their control. The first is to insist on calling the children by pet names given to them when they were little. But a name that showed affection to a small child becomes extremely irritating when applied to a teenager. You may find it hard to give up a name that has great sentimental significance for you, but you have to look at it from the youngster's perspective. How would *you* like to be called by the pet name you had when you were a small child?

Another thing adults do frequently is to recall 'amusing' incidents from their kids' early years and use them to entertain friends. They may also get out the family photo albums and insist on showing off all those 'cute' photos. You know the ones – the child sitting on a potty, or covering itself in jam. Parents will claim that this is all done 'in fun', but it's actually a subtle way of putting the child in its place and maintaining control. Kids hate this sort of thing, and they have every right to. Your parents probably did it to you, so you should remember how it feels. Have some sense, have some respect, and keep that photo album in a drawer where it belongs.

Personally, I have always found that my children have useful things to contribute. It was my son, not me, who worked out how to access the secret level in a video game I was playing; it was both my kids who warned us (correctly) that the 'nice young girl' we were about to employ as a babysitter was actually a rather dodgy character; and it was my daughter, though only thirteen, who provided some excellent illustrations for one of my books. It is important to recognise that though the kids may not be fully grown up in every way, they still deserve our respect. They may not know everything that experience has taught you about the ways of the world, but sometimes they are well ahead of you in some areas. You could save yourself a lot of trouble if you only had the sense to listen to them.

AN EMPTY NEST

The point at which the kids ought to leave home is the subject of much disagreement. At one extreme is the 'get to eighteen and you're out the door' lobby; at the other are the families in which the kids resolutely stay and make no effort to move out. There was even a TV ad recently in which a couple of elderly parents tentatively suggested to their middle-aged children that it might be time for them to set up on their own. The idea was met with blank incomprehension. It was supposed to be a joke, but, like all good jokes, it contained a kernel of truth.

> At 20 we worry about what others think of us; at 40 we
> don't care about what others think of us; at 60 we discover
> they haven't been thinking about us at all.
>
> *Anon.*

Some parents simply can't wait to get rid of the kids so that they can 'get their life back'. They look forward to a life without the noise and mess that seem to accompany teenagers and young adults wherever they go. They can then put the children's rooms to better use – at last they can have a proper spare room *and* a study. The strong desire to get rid of the kids is quite common. Once I even overheard a woman talking to her friend about her two children, who were seven and two years old. She said, 'I've already told them that when they get to eighteen they'll have to move out. My husband and I both left home at eighteen and we never went back.' On another occasion, a radio show was offering a bottle of champagne to the person who could suggest the best use for it. A number of people phoned in to say that they would open it to celebrate the departure of the last child from the family home.

At the other extreme are the people who simply cannot bear to lose their children and want to keep them at home for ever. Over the years they have relied on their children for companionship and help and they can't bear the thought of living alone. They do their best to discourage any signs of independence in their children and to drive away any prospective partners who might offer them a chance of a married life of their own. They don't necessarily do this consciously, or with malice aforethought, but nonetheless it's a selfish way to go about things for it proceeds at the expense of the child, who is condemned to a life more lonely and unfulfilled than it could have been.

Happily, most families fall somewhere between the extremes. For many of them the noise, mess and general mayhem that goes with having teenagers in the family is sometimes annoying but also makes for a lively household. Many feel that having kids around the place is one of the things that keeps them young. They also recognise, however, that at some point the kids will be grown up enough to leave home and that they must go if they are ever to become successful adults on their own account.

THE HIGHER EDUCATION BREAK

For children who are going on from school to colleges and universities there is a natural break with the family. It is probably the first time they have been away from home, but it is by no means a decisive split. College terms are quite short, for a start, and a student might easily end up spending twenty weeks of the year back at home. Still, it could prove to be a useful halfway house for both parents and children, allowing both parties to get used to a separation by stages – though these days, what with mobile phones, text messages, email and instant messaging, keeping in touch could not be simpler.

PROPERTY PRICES

Having become used to living away from home, your children may well wish to get a job and find somewhere to live. But rapidly rising property prices make buying a place impossible for many young people, and if they rent somewhere it makes saving for a deposit on a house extremely difficult. The result is that many of them are forced to go back home and live with their parents again.

This can be problematic. After maybe three years of partial separation both children and parents have learnt to enjoy their independence, yet now they are being forced to give it up. It will feel like a retrograde step. Also, the kids are not kids any more: they are now adults in their early twenties. They will naturally feel they can live their own lives, but because they are back in their parents' house they can't just do as they please.

> It takes a long time to become young.
>
> *Pablo Picasso*

The arrangement can and does work for many people, but in order to make it a success both parties have to be prepared to adapt to a new sort of relationship. After more than twenty years of having an adult–child relationship it can be hard to start behaving towards each other in an adult way. Some people slip into such an arrangement quite easily, but for others there may be a long period of adjustment. But it's well worth the effort to make the transition, because once it is established it makes for a much more harmonious future for all involved.

WHO NEEDS YOUR ADVICE?

There should be a law against people giving unsolicited advice. There are few things in the world quite as irritating as people who poke their nose into your affairs without permission. Parents and grandparents are the very worst offenders. What makes it even worse is that often they don't trouble to offer their opinions politely. Many parents and grandparents will say appallingly rude and hurtful things to their grown-up children that they would never dream of saying to any other adult, and then they quite fail to understand why they have made themselves unpopular.

Once your children are grown up, and especially if they are living with a partner, it is no longer your right to criticise or offer advice unless it is specifically asked for. No matter how much you might feel they are going about things the wrong way, you need to keep your lip firmly buttoned. This applies to every part of their life, from their appearance, their job and their home right down to their choice of partner. If you make it a habit to disapprove of what they do, even through facial expressions, manner and gesture rather than words, you will damage your relationship permanently. And the damage may not be obvious. Your children will probably continue to see you, but it will become a grim duty to be borne stoically rather than a pleasure to be warmly anticipated.

GRANDCHILDREN

If you're a grandparent, you need to be doubly careful. Don't you remember how protective you were of your children when they were little? Now it's their turn, and they feel just the same. Fashions in baby care change all the time. What was considered essential by one generation is regarded as foolishness by the next. If you try to interfere you are risking a major rift with your children. It is traditional for a mother to go and help her daughter with her newborn baby, but it is essential that you remember you are a guest in the home of another family. You are not there as an occupying army imposing its will on a subject nation. That may seem an extreme description, but in some cases it doesn't seem far short of the truth.

As soon as a newborn baby enters the picture a lot of very power-ful emotions come to the surface and people tend to act in strange ways. Grandparents often feel pangs of regret that they are no longer the proud parents but have been relegated to a subsidiary role. If they are sensible they will see that their new role is a very important one, but that it does *not* involve trying to rule the roost.

> The tendency of old age to the body, say the physiologists, is to form bone. It is as rare as it is pleasant to meet with an old man whose opinions are not ossified.
>
> *Bob Wells*

Grandparents frequently try to stick their noses into all sorts of matters that really don't concern them. For example, there is the vexed issue of naming the baby. If the parents *want* to call her Ermintrude, and you like Samantha, it's their decision, not yours. In any case, if your grandchild is anything like other kids she might junk the name and choose a new one when she reaches puberty. Similarly, it is up to the parents alone whether or not the baby is christened. This is an important and personal decision, and one that the grandparents should not be concerned with.

When the grandchildren are a little older you may well want to be very involved in looking after them. Their parents will by now have discovered just how much hard work is involved in bringing up a family and will be only too glad of your help, but only if they think they can trust you. You must learn the way they want their chil-dren brought up and comply with that. If you go behind their backs and treat the children in a wholly different way that happens to suit you, don't be surprised if a row erupts.

The best grandparents are regarded as a rock that underlies the whole fabric of the family; the worst are a constant irritant who cause their children nothing but trouble. One of the worst things old people can do is to use their age as a way of behaving badly with impunity. They know full well that younger people will avoid confrontation with them because no one wants to look like the sort of person who would bully an old person. We all know people who do this. So decide right now *never* to do such a thing!

Here are ten top tips for staying on the right path as a parent and grandparent:

1. Treat your children with the same respect you would give any other adult.
2. Don't offer advice unless you are asked for it.
3. Respect your children's opinions, even when you don't share them. Never assume that just because they are your children you must know better than they do.
4. Be aware that times change. What was done when you were young is not necessarily what is done now. Do not assume that such changes are always for the worse.
5. Be prepared to learn. Your children may be able to teach you a thing or two. Don't refuse to take them seriously just because they are your children.
6. Don't belittle your children – for example by telling embarrassing stories about their childhood. It can cause offence, and you may not know it.
7. If you have grandchildren, don't assume that because you were a parent you know all the answers. Accept that ideas about child rearing change.
8. By all means show your grandchildren affection, even spoil them a little, but don't encourage them to do things you know their parents would not allow, like letting them pig out on chocolate when their parents are trying to train them to eat fruit and vegetables.
9. Don't constantly remind your children of all you have done for them. If you were a good parent they will remember it without prompting.
10. Don't use your age as an excuse to behave badly and get away with it.

REDISCOVERING YOUR MARRIAGE

Instead of focusing on your children and/or grandchildren, why not concentrate your energies on renewing your relationship with your partner? The days when you were passionately in love with each other didn't last long, did they? Passion is very quickly extinguished by the responsibilities and cares of raising a family. But you loved each other once, or at any rate you decided to live together and produce children. Now, after 25 years or more, you find yourselves alone again. This is a huge change in your life, and it can take some getting used to.

> Those who love deeply never grow old; they may die of old age, but they die young.
>
> *Sir Arthur Wing Pinero*

Some couples have already discovered that they aren't happy but have stayed together for the sake of the children. As soon as the kids are off their hands they make straight for the nearest divorce lawyer and make a break for freedom. It is terribly sad to have spent the best years of your life in an unhappy relationship. Still, sometimes the split results in the couple being able to find new partners with whom they are more compatible. One couple I knew for many years always seemed rather grumpy and standoffish. I simply assumed they weren't particularly friendly people and left them alone. Suddenly, after their last child went to university, the wife moved out and a new partner moved in. The man underwent an almost magical transformation from a miserable fellow who would barely give you the time of day to a jolly, smiling man who was eager to make friendly contact with everybody around him. You got the feeling that he had just been let out of prison after a life sentence.

Happily, most couples have not become so estranged during their years of marriage. Even so, they may have got out of the habit of doing things together. Each may easily have evolved a lifestyle of his or her own, and now those lifestyles are threatened with radical change. Usually it is the wife who is more comfortable with being at home. She may well have worked part time and devoted quite a lot of her life to child-rearing. She may have an interesting and fulfilling life that does not involve her husband. It is not uncommon to hear women, when confronted with the prospect of a retired husband about the house, say, 'I don't want him at home getting under my feet all day!' The husband has his own problems. His life has centred on work and he now has nothing to do and loads of spare time in which to do it. He might have enjoyed a weekend game of golf with his friends but does not necessarily want to spend all his time down at the golf club.

> Age puzzles me. I thought it was a quiet time. My seventies were interesting and fairly serene, but my eighties are passionate. I grow more intense as I age.
> *Florida Scot-Maxwell*

If both partners are to have a happy life they need to adapt their lifestyle to the new conditions. Getting to know each other again will take some work, but it's a wonderful opportunity for rediscovering mutual interests or creating new ones. If you can see this period as an exciting chance to revitalise your lives, you stand a much better chance of continuing to make the relationship work.

Here are my ten top tips for staying together after the kids have flown the nest:

1. Try to remember what it was that you loved about each other when you were young. Ask yourself to what extent you have changed and how much of the magic still remains.
2. Don't take each other for granted. Show affection.
3. Develop new shared interests.
4. Don't just talk about petty everyday matters; make a point of communicating at a more profound level.
5. Give each other some space. If you are together all the time you are bound to get on each other's nerves.
6. Make plans for holidays and other adventures.
7. Share the household chores fairly.

8. Avoid bickering. When you have a problem, talk it through, come to an agreement, then forget it. Never go to bed without having made up.
9. We all have bad habits that irritate our partner. Make this the time you decide to get rid of them.
10. Never grow stale. Always look for new interests that will keep you lively.

Seven

Security Matters

It is a sad reflection on the values of modern society that some people see the elderly as chickens ripe for the plucking. It is not a pleasant topic to dwell on, especially in a book that concentrates on the positive aspects of ageing, but because crimes against older people are a daily occurrence it would be foolish not to discuss the subject. Of the elderly people known to me – and I know quite a few – there is not one who has not been duped or robbed at some time or other. Fortunately, none of these crimes involved any violence, but they all involved financial loss and great personal distress to the victims.

KNOCKS AT THE DOOR

The doorstep can be a dangerous place, and anyone approaching you there needs to be treated with suspicion. Those who prey on older people come in all shapes and sizes, and you have to be ready for them. At the bottom end of the scale are unscrupulous gardeners, window cleaners, electricians, plumbers, handymen and others who make a practice of overcharging elderly customers. They sometimes pretend that they have spotted something dangerously wrong with your house – loose tiles on the roof, for example – and they offer to carry out repairs before disaster strikes. Often they even have the cheek to tell you that they are charging you a 'special price'. They are – it's an especially high price, based on the hope that you won't know what the job is worth.

> As we grow older we grow both more foolish and wiser at the same time.
>
> *François de la Rochefoucauld*

There are three things everybody, no matter what their age, should do:

- Make a practice of *never* doing business with people who call at the door. People engaged in a proper business don't operate that way. They advertise their services and wait for customers to come to them.
- Always get competitive quotes in writing for any work you have done. All tradesmen are accustomed to being asked to quote for work. You should detail exactly what work you want done and agree a price in advance. Even then you need to remain wary because sometimes tradesmen will agree to what seems like a reasonable price only to discover hidden snags (sometimes imaginary) once they have started the

work. The snags will, of course, mean padding the bill considerably.

- If at all possible, you should hire people who have been recommended to you as being competent and honest.

And there are all sorts of other ways in which unsuspecting victims can be robbed.

DEALERS

Some people offer to buy articles for ready cash. If you let them in they will be on the lookout for antiques, coins, medals and any other valuables you might have. While offering you a price that is well below market value, they will tell you just what a wonderful deal you are getting. The main inducement they have is the offer of ready cash in return for your valuables, and there is never a shortage of older people willing to accept such offers.

If subsequently you find out that you have been cheated there is very little you can do about it as no actual crime has taken place, so the only safeguard is never to sell anything to casual callers. If you really want to sell things you should first have them properly valued so that when you sell privately you know what price to ask. Alternatively, you should sell by auction where the bidding process will usually ensure that you get a fair price.

BOGUS OFFICIALS

You also need to look out for bogus officials pretending that they are from the gas board, the electricity company, the council, etc. They will sound very plausible, but you mustn't let them in before you have checked their ID. *All* officials now carry ID cards. These not only give the name and photo of the carrier but should also give a phone number where that person's story can be checked out. Don't worry about appearing rude as proper officials know the rules and are happy to abide by them. If anyone tries to persuade you not to make that phone call you need to be very suspicious of their motives.

> Wisdom doesn't necessarily come with age.
> Sometimes age just shows up all by itself.
>
> *Tom Wilson*

CON MEN

Confidence tricksters are particularly interested in elderly victims. They will always appear to be pleasant, affable types who are the very model of respectability. The danger is that many elderly people are rather lonely and welcome the chance to have a chat with someone who seems so nice.

At some point they will start to persuade you to take part in some financial scheme or other. There are so many dodgy deals that it would take another book to describe them all, but they have one feature in common: they all involve you handing over money to the con man.

Don't for a moment think that you are a good judge of character and will be able to spot a shady operator when you see one. These people are good at what they do. There have been many cases where, even after the crook was unmasked and jailed, his victims have found it hard to believe that such a 'nice young man' was really duping them.

THIEVES

Thieves prey on older people because it's easy. Sometimes a pair of them will call at the door with a plausible story to persuade you to let them in. While one engages your attention by chatting pleasantly, the other will slip upstairs on the lookout for any money, jewellery or other valuables you might have. Other thieves simply throw all caution to the winds and smash a window or kick in a door to gain entry.

There is no end to the ways in which unscrupulous people take advantage of the elderly. Recently there was a case widely reported in the press of an old lady living alone who could no longer climb the stairs and was therefore forced to live on the ground floor of her house. Her children became concerned that she seemed to be drinking too much because bottles of sherry seemed to become empty far too quickly. The old lady denied having a drink problem, so her children became even more worried. Eventually an explanation was found. A young woman had moved into the upper storey of the house and had been living there undetected for several months. She had also been coming down at night when the old lady was asleep and had helped herself to anything she found there, including the sherry.

STAYING SAFE

You should contact your local police station and ask for the crime prevention officer to call on you. He will be able to assess your risk and point out any areas that are especially vulnerable. Here are some of the most obvious precautions you should take:

- You need to guard your front door well as it is the likeliest route for crooks to approach you. Have a good, strong lock fitted, and add bolts at the top and bottom. Insert a spyhole and keep a security chain on the door when you open it to anyone you don't know. To find a good locksmith you need to consult the *Yellow Pages*, or ask friends and family for recommendations. You'll find that having this sort of work done is not cheap and you may have to shop around to get the best deal, but don't be tempted to save money on a cheap lock because that will prove to be a false economy.
- All the windows should have locks on them too, and you need to remember to lock them at night. You are particularly vulnerable during the summer when people leave windows and doors open to let air in. If you aren't careful you will get more than a cool breeze entering your house.
- In the garden, be sure not to leave ladders and tools lying around. A thief will be only too willing to put any of your tools to good use when breaking into your house. You might also find that your insurance company will be less willing to pay out if they discover that the break-in was helped by your carelessness.
- A crime prevention officer might also advise you to lay gravel on your driveway so that anyone approaching the house will make a noise, or grow prickly plants such as brambles near or on boundary walls, or in parts of the garden where intruders might try to force an entry.

Sir Alec Guinness

Alec Guinness was born in 1914 and was destined to become a world-famous actor. It was always said that part of his success was that he had the sort of face you could pass in a crowd without recognizing. His rather bland looks enabled him to assume a character almost like putting on a mask. He decided to try movies, and worked with the director David Lean on *Bridge on the River Kwai* (for which he was awarded an Oscar), *Lawrence of Arabia*, *Doctor Zhivago* and *Great Expectations*. He also played Fagin in *Oliver Twist*. By 1949 he was getting to be well known and featured in the Ealing comedies *Kind Hearts and Coronets* – famous for the fact that Guinness played eight different characters, a feat that brought him instant fame – and *The Lavender Hill Mob*. He was knighted in 1959, and in his sixties he played the sage Jedi knight Ben Obi-Wan Kenobi in the hit movie *Star Wars* and its sequels. On stage and television he was also a popular and critical success, notably in *Tinker, Tailor, Soldier, Spy*. One of his last films, *Little Dorrit*, made when he was 73, earned him yet another Oscar nomination.

CCTV AND LIGHTING

Closed-circuit television is an excellent way to keep watch over your property and deter thieves. A small camera fixed outside your house will monitor people approaching your home. The camera is wired to your TV and you can see visitors on screen without having to open the door. A basic system is cheap and very easy to fit. If you wish, you can buy more sophisticated systems with more than one camera. This should act as a deterrent, but even if it doesn't you will have some video footage of the culprits to give to the police. You should also have a security light that comes on whenever someone approaches the house. All these things can be bought from your local DIY store, and you will probably be able to fit them yourself. If not, you can get a local electrician to do it for you.

I think age is a very high price to pay for maturity.
Tom Stoppard

BURGLAR ALARMS

There is a wide variety of burglar alarms on the market. The cheapest are little battery-operated sensors that detect the infrared light generated by the heat of a human body. You just screw these to a wall so that they cover all possible points of entry. If during the night anyone comes within range of the sensors they let out a high-pitched wail that will wake you up and, with luck, scare off the thieves. This sort of alarm is cheap to buy at your local DIY store and you can fit it in minutes yourself. If you want to, you can pay out for a more sophisticated system with more sensors. These are still not very expensive, and as long as you are reasonably competent at DIY you will be able to fit them yourself.

SECURITY SYSTEMS

There is no limit to the sophistication of security systems. You can pay thousands of pounds to have your property protected by invisible laser beams linked to alarm systems that will summon the police if they are set off. There are also companies that will provide alarms that not only detect intruders and outbreaks of fire but will also alert the emergency services automatically. This sort of protection is very expensive, but if you live in an area where there is a lot of crime you might consider it money well spent.

Finding security companies could not be easier. It sometimes seems that every policeman who retires immediately starts up a private security firm. Look up 'Security' in the *Yellow Pages* and you will be amazed at the number of firms advertising there.

How do you pick a good security company? Again, personal recommendation is the best way, but it is not always possible. Your best chance is to pick out a few companies and ask them to quote. People who try to sell you a very complicated and expensive system that is clearly more than you need should be discarded straight away. Try to find someone who is happy to offer you a system that you can afford, and which seems adequate for your purposes.

IF THE WORST SHOULD HAPPEN

In truth, nothing you do will prevent a determined and skilful crook from getting into your house, but the great majority of thieves are opportunists, and if you don't give them an easy chance they'll go elsewhere.

If the worst happens and you do find yourself face to face with a thief, *give them the money*. Don't, under any circumstances, decide to 'have a go'. The tabloids may love the sort of story where a battling granny drives off her attacker by belting him with her handbag, but it is not generally a good idea. If all you stand to lose is money, then lose it. There is no point in risking a beating or a heart attack just to protect the contents of your purse. Also, remember that if you injure your attacker seriously it may be you and not him who ends up facing charges of assault. You don't want to go down for GBH at your age, do you?

FIRE PRECAUTIONS

Crime is not the only thing you need to take precautions against. There is also the risk of fire. You need to fit smoke alarms, upstairs and downstairs, that are powerful enough to wake you when they go off, and they need to be fitted in places where a fire is most likely to start. If you don't have a fire the alarm will remain unused for years, so you need to check regularly that the batteries are fully charged and the alarm still works. Most of them have a test button that allows you to do this.

You also need to think out in advance how you would get out of the house if a fire started at night. A contingency plan saves you losing valuable time working out which is the quickest exit while the house is on fire.

In the event of fire, you are more likely to be killed by the smoke than the flames, so you need to stay low. The smoke is hot and will therefore rise, leaving clearer air beneath it. This situation won't last very long because soon there will be so much smoke that it fills the whole house, but by staying low you can gain vital seconds in which to make your escape. If possible, you should put a wet cloth over your nose and mouth to stave off the fumes.

> Live your life and forget your age.
>
> *Norman Vincent Peale*

OTHER HAZARDS

There are other hazards around the house that cause injuries, even to much younger people. Slippery floors, loose carpets and rugs, electrical wires left trailing across floors, and loose stair carpets are all potential hazards. All these things can produce a nasty fall, and as you get older, falls can have serious consequences. Have a look around your house, spot areas of potential danger, and do something to eliminate the problem.

Once you are that bit older, jobs that involve a degree of risk, such as climbing ladders, should be left to others. Older people like to think they are just as capable as they ever were, and on the whole this is a good thing. But it is just as well to know your limits and avoid unnecessary risks. If you insist on doing this sort of thing yourself then at least make sure you have the right equipment. Don't try to put a coat of emulsion on the ceiling while standing on some rickety old kitchen stool; get a set of steps that will take your weight and won't slip out from under you.

OTHER PRECAUTIONS

If you have good neighbours you should give them a spare key to your house so that they can get in if there's an emergency while you're away. You should also have a mobile phone (or a cordless phone) so that you can keep it with you and call someone.

If you are on your own, you could make sure that someone looks out for you and notices if you are not around. If you were to have an accident and for any reason you couldn't use your phone, then at least you'd know that eventually you'd be missed. There is also a scheme in which you wear a small alarm around your neck, a bit like a pendant. If you have an accident or become ill and can't get to the phone, you simply press the panic button on your alarm and help will be sent.

When you go out, you should make sure you have something with you that contains your name, address and next of kin so that if anything should happen the right person is informed straight away. If you have a mobile, make sure you charge regularly it, take it with you and leave it switched on. Most of us born in the frugal 1950s were taught from infancy that it's wasteful to keep electrical gadgets switched on when they are not in use, but the whole point of a mobile is that it should be on all the time. This way you can be contacted at any time by relatives or friends who are anxious to know your whereabouts.

If you don't know how to send a text message, find out. It is very easy, and it is a quick, cheap way to keep in touch. In a text you can let someone know in a few words where you are, what you're doing, and what time you intend to arrive. Texting only works if you keep your phone on all the time. When a text message arrives, your mobile lets you know by making a sound (some of them vibrate as well). Text messages cost a fraction of the price of a phone call and they are just as effective for many purposes.

All this may sound frightening, but prevention is always better than cure. If you spend some time and effort making sure that you and your home are well protected, you should be able to enjoy life safe in the knowledge that the bad guys will be put off by your precautions and will leave you alone.

Eight

The Final Curtain

This book started with the proposition that there are many things we can do to stave off decay and extend our lifespan. This is a battle well worth fighting, but one that we are, of course, eventually going to lose. In spite of all the remarkable advances of medical science, the mortality rate remains at 100 per cent. This is not a subject we like to think about, but we struggle to ignore it.

> People like you and I, though mortal of course like everyone else, do not grow old no matter how long we live . . . [We] never cease to stand like curious children before the great mystery into which we were born.
> *Albert Einstein (in a letter to Otto Juliusburger)*

In former times death was commonplace and not merely confined mostly to the very old as children were also quite frequently carried off by disease. In contrast, I was recently talking with a group of middle-aged friends when one of them remarked just how much she would hate to see a dead body. Immediately the others agreed, and it turned out that they had all lived to the age of 40 or 50 without ever having seen anyone dead. A generation ago this would have seemed inconceivable.

There used to be well-established rites and practices that helped people come to terms with death. Now we have a much more arms'-length attitude to the whole subject. It isn't just that we find it unsettling, we are also embarrassed by it because we are unsure how to behave when someone dies. People who have been bereaved often find that friends and acquaintances avoid them, not out of callousness but simply because they have no idea what to say or how to behave. I remember as a very young man going to the funeral of my aunt. When it came to greeting my cousin I went through agonies trying to decide whether to smile to show I was pleased to see him or to keep a straight face in keeping with the solemnity of the occasion.

But all of us must face death, if only to make sure that certain practical matters have been arranged and are watertight.

ENDURING POWER OF ATTORNEY

We all like to hope that when our time comes, death will be quick and painless. Nobody wants to contemplate a long, lingering illness that robs us of our faculties bit by bit. The truth, however, is that such things do happen, and if they do we should be prepared.

An enduring power of attorney is a document drawn up by a solicitor that stipulates that if, in the opinion of two doctors, you are no longer in a fit state to govern your own affairs, power of attorney will be granted to a person (or persons) of your choice. Most commonly, people choose to nominate their eldest child, but you can choose anyone who you think will handle the job best and who is willing to take on this responsibility.

Because people hate to talk about these matters not many of them are even aware that such an agreement is possible. If you become incapable of making decisions and you have not appointed anyone to this crucial role then you risk your family becoming involved in all sorts of difficulties. There is also the prospect that various members of the family will quarrel over who should be making the decisions on your behalf.

An enduring power of attorney is quite simple to draw up. It takes very little time, it's not expensive, and it makes sure that your affairs will be properly handled.

> If we don't know life, how can we know death?
>
> *Confucius*

A LIVING WILL

Like the enduring power of attorney, a living will is made long before it is needed. It need not be a formal document, though it is safer to put it in writing. The living will stipulates what is to be done if your condition becomes really desperate. Specifically, it deals with the issue of resuscitation. Unless you stipulate otherwise, doctors are obliged to keep you alive by all means at their disposal. This may mean that they repeatedly try to resuscitate you even though your life is, to all intents and purposes, over. By making a living will you relieve the doctors and your family of an agonising decision. If you state plainly that you do not want to be resuscitated then there can be no argument and no pangs of guilt for the relatives.

You should also make it clear to your next of kin where you stand on the subject of organ donation. If you want your organs to be used for transplants, you need to make sure that those close to you know that is your view. Some people are happy to have certain organs transplanted but not others. For example, a lot of people who are quite content to donate their heart or lungs feel squeamish about having their corneas removed. This may be irrational, but if it is the way you feel then you have every right to have your wishes observed. Some people want to leave their whole body to be used for dissection by medical students. This is a subject that makes many people shudder and turn away, but if this is your wish you have to make it absolutely clear to your relatives.

> Death is one moment, and life is so many of them.
> *Tennessee Williams*

THE WILL

Making a will is a simple business, but huge numbers of people don't do it, either because they have a superstitious fear of anything to do with death or because they think they have so little to leave that it's not worth the bother. This is quite misguided. Every adult should make a will, but especially people who own a house and have a family. It is important that you make your wishes quite clear by spelling them out in a formal document.

It is possible to buy a will form and do it yourself, but it is far better to go to a solicitor and have the whole thing done properly. If you are not familiar with legal niceties it's quite easy to leave loopholes in something you thought was watertight. And getting your will drawn up by a solicitor need not be expensive. Unless you have a family solicitor you always use, ask for a recommendation or trawl through the *Yellow Pages* and make a few phone calls. These days solicitors are not so coy about their charges as they used to be. You can expect them to quote you a flat fee for the job, and you can get quotes from as many companies as you want.

If you make your will while you are still young you must not simply address the problem of what happens to your estate when you die, you should also make it clear who it is you wish to look after your children if you and your partner were to die at the same time. There could hardly be a more important decision. Naturally, you need to consult whoever you nominate and make sure that they are willing to undertake this enormous responsibility. You might also want to leave them all or part of your estate to cover the expenses they will incur – bringing up children, as the majority of us have found out, is not a cheap business. It's a difficult subject, which is why many people prefer simply to trust to luck and hope that the circumstances never arise. Sadly, sometimes they do, so the future happiness of your children will depend on you having made a wise choice.

> People living deeply have no fear of death.
>
> *Anais Nin*

Your will can be as simple or as complicated as you wish. Most people simply leave the bulk of their estate to a surviving partner. You might also want to make some bequests to old friends, or to leave a legacy to your favourite charity. But if your situation is more complicated than that you need the help of a solicitor to ensure that your wishes are carried out. For example, if you have married twice and you have children by both partners, the division of the estate could be quite complicated. Unless you are quite clear about what you want to do, you could leave a legacy of family strife for years to come.

If you are not married to the person you live with, or if you are a same-sex couple, then you cannot automatically assume that your assets will pass to that person unless you clearly stipulate that that is what you want to happen. There have been many cases where the person closest to the deceased is elbowed out of the way by blood relatives on the basis that they are next of kin. If you want to avoid such a thing, you need to set it all down in your will.

AN EXECUTOR

One of the most important parts of making your will is to nominate an executor to take responsibility for carrying out all your instructions and to deal with the various officials who are concerned with the estate. If you have a lawyer or accountant in the family then he or she might be the natural choice. If not, then you need to choose someone whose common sense and organising abilities you trust. Being an executor is a great responsibility, so you must approach the person and make sure that they find this duty acceptable.

If you have no one you would want to be your executor, your bank will do the job. Beware, however, that banks charge a lot of money for this service, and their fee will take a chunk out of the money you hoped to leave.

CODICILS

It is possible that over the years you may think of minor alterations you would like to make to your will. For example, you may have grandchildren and wish to leave them a separate bequest. Rather than go to the trouble and expense of drafting a new will from scratch you can add a codicil to the original document. Your solicitor will be happy to do this for you.

> He who fears death enjoys not life.
>
> *Anon.*

WHAT DO YOU DO WHEN SOMEONE DIES?

This is an area in which a surprising number of people are almost entirely unschooled. The following list will help you to remember your responsibilities at a time when you may find it hard to think clearly. When someone close to you dies:

- If your loved one died in hospital, go to collect personal effects.
- Establish whether a post-mortem is needed.
- Establish whether there is to be an inquest.
- You must get a medical certificate from the doctor who last treated the deceased.
- Inform close relatives by phone.
- Find the will and any other important papers (e.g. bank books and insurance policies).
- Go to the register office to register the death.
- Contact a funeral director and arrange details for the ceremony.
- Decide who is to conduct the funeral service and meet him/her to discuss who will speak or give readings.
- Announce the death to the world at large by phone, letter or newspaper notice. Make sure you also give the date and place of the funeral and any wishes concerning flowers or charitable donations.
- If the will is complicated, the solicitor will want to read it in front of all those concerned, so an appointment needs to be made.
- Arrange the provision of refreshments after the funeral.

Most of these duties are self-explanatory, but a few require a bit more information.

REGISTERING A DEATH

You have a legal obligation to register the death, and to do this you must go to the local register office. There are a number of things you need to bring:

- the medical certificate of the cause of death;
- the deceased's medical card, birth and marriage certificates, if you have them;
- any relevant documents if the deceased was receiving a pension or allowance (e.g. disability or benefit payments) from public funds;
- any insurance policies owned by the deceased;
- notification from the coroner in cases where there was a post-mortem.

The registrar will want to know the following:

- date and place of birth and death;
- address and full name (and, where appropriate, maiden name);
- occupation and the name, date of birth and occupation of spouse;
- details of any pension or other social security benefits.

You need to get from the registrar a certificate for burial or cremation, which you should take to the funeral director. You also need a certificate of registration of death for social security purposes. If this applies, you should fill it in and send it to your local social security office. You can also ask the registrar about widow benefits and income tax for widows, if this is appropriate. The death certificate is a copy of the entry made by the registrar on the death register. If you need a death certificate for pension or insurance claims, you will be charged a fee by the registrar.

THE FUNERAL

Few occasions provide more opportunity for family disagreements than a funeral. The relatives gather round, and all have their own opinions about exactly what sort of service there should be, whether mourners should send flowers or make a donation to charity, who should travel in which of the funeral cars, what music should be played, and what sort of hospitality ought to be offered to those who stay on after the service has ended. Everyone will back up his or her opinion with that time-worn phrase, 'I'm sure it's what he/she would have wanted.' For some reason, everybody involved with a funeral seems to develop a telepathic link with the deceased through which their last wishes are clearly communicated.

> It is not death, it is dying that alarms me.
> *Michel de Montaigne*

If you want to avoid your funeral turning into a free-for-all among your nearest and dearest, you need to plan it in advance. Here are a number of points to consider.

- What sort of funeral do you want? If you belong to a religious faith, you need to select which church, temple or mosque you wish the service to be held at.
- Do you want to be buried or cremated? If you opt for cremation, what is to be done with your ashes afterwards? Will you ask your family to keep them in an urn on the mantelpiece, or will you have them scattered on the pitch of the football team you supported for 50 years? These days there are a couple of other choices open to you. You could be buried in a woodland burial site, which is unlike a formal cemetery and which some people feel is rather more aesthetically pleasing than endless rows of marble slabs. If you have strong views on the environment, you might consider being buried in a cardboard coffin that rots quickly, as opposed to the ecologically less satisfactory practice of using a wooden coffin.
- Do you wish your body to be embalmed? The funeral directors will arrange that, but, as it costs extra, they won't do it unless they have specific instructions.
- Do you have any other special wishes? If you want to be buried in your favourite football shirt or your favourite suit, you need to say so. If you want your wedding ring to accompany you to the other side, you must leave specific instructions.
- These days, people are allowed quite a lot of latitude in deciding what sort of funeral service they have. If instead of the 23rd Psalm you want Bob Dylan singing 'Knocking on

Heaven's Door', there's no reason why you shouldn't get what you want – again, as long as you have made your wishes clear.

- How is the funeral to be paid for? You have no doubt seen all those annoying TV commercials which encourage you to start saving for 'those last expenses'. Like most people, you are thoroughly fed up of having well-known actors remind you that you're going to die. Unfortunately, they do have a point. Someone will have to foot the bill for the funeral and you need to ensure that whoever it is will be adequately compensated.

- After the funeral it is usual to invite close friends and relatives to come back to the house, or some other venue, for refreshments. Often people have travelled a long way to be there so it is polite to offer them some hospitality before they face the return journey. Unless you have someone who is willing and able to handle the refreshments for you it will be necessary to choose a caterer.

The bottom line is that you can have just about any type of funeral you want, as long as you make sure that all those involved know your wishes. (And you have to have some sort of funeral; you can't opt simply to be chucked in a hole without ceremony. If you are of no particular faith you are likely to end up with an off-the-peg Church of England funeral.) This means that you have to spend some time thinking about what you want. Almost everybody tries to avoid thinking about these matters because they are unpleasant to contemplate, but it is far better to do it in advance and make sure that your arrangements are as you want them than to have to worry about such things when you are terminally ill, or, even worse, not to have any time to think about them at all.

George Burns

For sheer longevity, it's hard to beat the American comedian George Burns. He was born Nathan Birbaum in 1896, the ninth of twelve children. His second wife, Gracie Allen, became his partner, and together they formed a double act that had a huge following on both sides of the Atlantic. Gracie's role was the scatterbrained housewife while George smoked his trademark cigar and made droll asides to the audience. She died in 1964, and he never remarried. He did carry on with his career, however, and was always a popular stand-up comedian. In later years his age was a running gag. He would say, 'I'd go out with women of my own age but there *are* no women my age.' Another typical remark was, 'This job gets easier the older you get. Once I had to walk on to the stage and tell jokes to get applause, but nowadays I get the applause just for making it on to the stage.' George lived to be 100 and was active as an entertainer right up to the end.

BEREAVEMENT

What if someone close to you dies before you do? If death itself is a taboo subject, then the idea of being left behind by a much-loved partner or friend is a thought most of us shrink from completely. It is tragic but true that nearly every marriage will end this way. Moreover, as we grow older some of our friends will also die before we do.

> Our life is made by the death of others.
>
> *Leonardo da Vinci*

Bereavement always comes as a huge shock. If someone dies suddenly having shown no previous signs of ill health, it is easy to see how those left behind will be shaken by the suddenness of such a sad event. However, those who lose someone after a long illness, though they may think they have had a chance to prepare themselves for the worst, are often taken by surprise when the end actually comes.

Being in a state of shock is not only distressing but dangerous. It is very important at such times to have someone with you who is less involved and who can look after you during those difficult days just after the event. Your mental processes simply do not function properly at such times and you will be forgetful, clumsy and accident prone while your mind tries to come to terms with what has happened. If you are deeply distressed your doctor may prescribe sedatives. Because these will make you sleep deeply for long periods, it is especially important to have someone to look after you.

It is not unusual for someone recently bereaved to hear or even see their loved one. This has nothing to do with ghosts, it is simply a trick of the mind that is trying hard to cope with a loss that is difficult to accept.

THE FIRST THINGS TO DO

At a time when you are feeling at your lowest ebb there are practical tasks that have to be carried out (see 'What do you do when someone dies?' on page 216). If you are too distressed to do this you will need a relative or friend to help.

If your loved one died suddenly, there may need to be a post-mortem. If there is any doubt over the circumstances of the death there may also have to be an inquest at which the coroner will summon witnesses and try to establish how the death happened. In cases where there is real doubt about the cause of death the body may not be released for burial until the coroner is satisfied that all the necessary information is available. Fortunately, such cases are rare; usually there is nothing to prevent the family making arrangements for the funeral.

Your first duty, of course, is to visit the hospital and pick up the deceased person's personal effects. This can be very distressing. At any one time there may be several recent deaths in the hospital and to see all the personal effects lined up in labelled bin liners awaiting collection is extremely unpleasant. Fortunately, the process is a quick one. You sign for the effects and take your bag straight away.

> I see no comfort in outliving one's friends, and remaining a mere monument of the times which are past.
>
> *Thomas Jefferson*

FUNERAL ARRANGEMENTS

You will need to contact a funeral director who will help you either to implement your partner's wishes concerning his/her funeral, or to choose the sort of funeral you want (see 'The funeral' on page 217). If the latter, at a time when you are feeling particularly helpless there are many decisions to be made, but funeral directors are used to this and are good at putting the relatives at ease and helping them through what is bound to be a very distressing process.

Almost everybody feels that arranging and attending the funeral of a loved one is an enormous strain, but at the same time it does mark an official, respectful conclusion to the deceased's life which allows the relatives the chance to get back to normality and start the process of rebuilding their lives. Funerals are very varied and you really do need to work closely with the funeral director to make sure that the ceremony is exactly right.

Firstly, you will need to decide what to do with the body prior to the funeral. Is it to be left in the hospital mortuary or moved to a chapel of rest? Do you, your family and friends want to view the body before burial? The hospital will have given you the chance to see your loved one shortly after death, but now you have to decide whether you want to have a final visit before the funeral. Personal reactions vary. Some people feel they would rather keep in mind the way their relative looked just after death when the body was still warm and it was as if he or she were merely sleeping. Others put a great deal of emphasis on seeing the body to say a final goodbye. In some countries – the USA and Ireland, for example – viewing the body is an important part of the grieving process and allows everyone a chance to pay their last respects. If you find the decision difficult, you should talk it over with the funeral director and get his or her advice.

The funeral director will also want to discuss issues such as:

- burial or cremation (and what to do with the ashes, if the latter);
- the type of coffin you want;
- the type of headstone, and the inscription to go on it;
- the number of funeral cars;
- location of the funeral and burial.

THE CELEBRANT

Before the funeral, you will also need to talk with whoever is conducting the service. If you are a regular member of some faith community the problem is easily solved. If you are not, then you will have to find someone to conduct the service for you. The funeral director should be able to help out by suggesting suitable people.

Whoever is to conduct the ceremony will want to visit you before the day, talk about the deceased and get enough information for the eulogy. In this short speech it is usual to talk of the deceased's good qualities and his or her contributions to the family and the world at large.

The celebrant will also need to agree an order of service with you. You need to choose any readings from scripture, poems, hymns, songs or music that will be included. You might also choose to have friends or relatives give some of the readings, or make a short speech of their own. You might, if you feel up to it, decide to speak yourself.

> I believe that imagination is stronger than knowledge – myth is more potent than history – dreams are more powerful than facts – hope always triumphs over experience – laughter is the cure for grief – love is stronger than death.
>
> *Robert Fulghum*

TELLING PEOPLE

You also need to let as many people as possible know of your loss. The worst part of this is phoning all your relatives and friends. It means that you have to go over an extremely harrowing experience again and again. You may want to get a family member – one of your children, perhaps – to help out with the task.

Then there is the job of letting the wider world know.

- People who were close to the deceased, such as personal friends or work colleagues, need to be told individually. You can either include them in your list of phone calls or send out a letter or card giving the sad news. Inevitably, people will phone you as soon as they hear what has happened so you need to be prepared to go over the whole story many more times.
- You should also write to any societies, clubs or organisations that need to be told.
- You also need to inform banks, building societies, solicitors and official bodies such as Inland Revenue. If all your bank and building society accounts were in joint names you will have no problems getting access to your money, but if any of

them were in the sole name of the deceased you will be unable to touch this money until you have probate (see page 227).

Broadcasting the news of a death is both time-consuming and distressing, but the more thorough you are the better it will be for you. It is far more distressing after the funeral to keep receiving letters, phone calls or emails addressed to the deceased. Having to go back to people and tell them the news just as you have started to feel a bit better is an experience to be avoided.

Death notice

You should also put a death notice in the local newspaper and, if your loved one had a very wide circle of acquaintants, you might want to put a notice in one of the national dailies. The death notice includes not simply an announcement of the death but should also say where and when the funeral is to be held. Then you have to show where you stand on the issue of floral tributes. Some people like flowers at a funeral; others feel they are a completely pointless gesture. If you don't want flowers it is usual to nominate a favourite charity to ask for contributions to be sent there. It is common but by no means compulsory to nominate a charity that deals with people suffering from whatever disease your loved one died from.

> If you live to be 100, you've got it made. Very few people die past that age.
>
> *George Burns*

COPING WITH GRIEF

Grief is a strange emotion. After the initial shock, however sad you're feeling your mind is capable of coping for at least some of the time. Most people describe grief as coming over them in waves. They seem to be coping quite well, but every now and then they are completely bowled off by a dreadful feeling of loss that leaves them helpless.

Given this, and as this is a time when you are called upon to make important decisions even though you feel at your lowest ebb, don't try to do all this on your own. You really need the support of a relative or friend, and if possible, that person should come to stay with you for a while until you feel able to carry on without help.

Most people feel that the funeral is an enormous ordeal and that once it is over life can start to return to normal. That is not, in my experience, quite true. From the first shock of death right up to the funeral itself you are propelled by pure adrenalin. A death is a weird form of excitement that forces us to great efforts and fills our days with decisions, preparations and plans. Then, quite suddenly, it is all over. Everybody returns to their normal lives and carries on as before – except that in your life there is now a great hole where someone used to be. This sudden feeling of emptiness is in many ways worse than the intense feelings of grief that preceded it.

Although at the time it is common to feel that you will never recover from your grief, you probably will. That does not mean that you will ever forget the deceased person, or the time you spent together, but you will eventually find that the pain subsides. This can take a year or so, but in the vast majority of cases it will happen.

If after six months or so you still feel no better you may be suffering from clinical depression (see page 132), and should consult your doctor. There is also help available for the bereaved through an organisation called Cruise Bereavement Care. You can contact them on tel: 0870 167 1677, or email them at helpline@cruisebereavementcare.org.uk.

PROBATE

Tidying up someone's estate – money, property and possessions – can be a painstaking and time-consuming business, but it has to be done. Normally the executor – the person who has undertaken to carry out the instructions left in the will – is the person who will seek probate. To do this, he or she must:

- collect all monies, including any still owed to the deceased;
- pay off any debts;
- divide the estate between the people who are entitled to it, or according to the will.

The probate registry is responsible for sending out a legal document called a grant of representation which allows one or more people to deal with the estate. This is what is called getting probate. You need a grant of probate so that various bodies holding the deceased's money will release it to you. Also, there are things you need to do, such as sell the deceased's house, which will be impossible unless you have probate.

There are rules governing who may be given a grant:

- If there is a will with named executors, they are the first people entitled to a grant.
- If there are no executors, or the executors are unable or unwilling to apply, the next person entitled to a grant is any person named in the will to whom the estate or remainder of it, after gifts have been paid, has been given.
- If the deceased has not made a will, application for a grant should normally be made by his or her next of kin in the following order of priority:

  1. Lawful husband or wife (NB: common-law partners have no entitlement to a grant).

2. Sons or daughters (or, if any have died in the lifetime of the deceased, their children may apply).
3. Parents.
4. Brothers or sisters (or, if any have died in the lifetime of the deceased, their children may apply).
5. Grandparents.
6. Uncles or aunts (or, if any have died in the lifetime of the deceased, their children may apply).

A grant cannot be issued to any person under the age of eighteen.

WHEN YOU DON'T NEED PROBATE

Where an estate is held entirely in joint names, probate will not be necessary. There may also be some cases – for example, where the estate is a small one – where some bodies are willing to release money without probate. It is worth approaching each of the bodies holding money to ask whether or not they require probate before releasing money to you.

> There is no such thing as old age, there is only sorrow.
> *Fay Weldon*

INHERITANCE TAX

What used to be called death duty is now known as inheritance tax, and it is levied on estates of a certain size. At the time of writing (2004), that tax threshold stands at £263,000. If the entire value of the estate exceeds this figure then tax is charged at 40% on any amount above the threshold.

This is a political hot potato at the moment. Inheritance tax was always intended to be a tax on the wealthy. However, because we have had a period of price inflation in the property market many people who would never be regarded as rich now live in houses that are worth well over a quarter of a million pounds. Naturally, many are bitter that they are being taxed heavily on what is actually a rather modest estate. Discussions are continuing, and it may be that the threshold will be raised in future, but for the moment, if you inherit you will find that the Inland Revenue demands its cut.

If you want further information on tax, you can approach your local Inland Revenue office, or look at the website (www.inlandrevenue.gov.uk). For all matters arising from the winding up of someone's estate there is excellent information at www.courtservice.gov.uk.

Afterword: The power of the internet

WHAT'S THE USE OF COMPUTERS?

There's a TV advert for computers that shows a family going into the showroom to buy their first PC. The father looks on with a gormless expression on his face while the kids get to grips with the machine and the mother smiles proudly at her youngsters' computer skills.

Sadly, there is an element of truth in all this. Anyone above the age of 30 was schooled in a world prior to the advent of home computers and the internet, so they did not have the advantage of being educated in computer literacy. Many have either educated themselves in the mysteries of computing or have taken courses to bring them up to speed. For others, however, the whole subject of IT is a closed book.

This is a great pity, because computers are just as useful to the old as they are to the young. You can use them to write letters, pay bills, keep track of finances, and perform hundreds of other useful tasks more quickly and conveniently than ever before. People who have learnt to use computers cannot imagine how they ever managed without them.

AM I TOO OLD TO LEARN?

People over 50, in particular, are completely polarised in their attitude to new technology. There is plenty of evidence that many thousands of 'silver surfers', as they are called, are happy to use the internet for everything from online shopping to getting health advice or keeping in touch with their friends. But there remains a hardcore of people for whom technology is a forbidding thing.

There is a false perception among some older people that all this new technology is simply too new and too complicated for them ever to understand.

In fact, you can learn to perform basic tasks on a home computer with very little instruction. In recent years, computers have become much more user-friendly: for example, the one I'm using as I write this is busy correcting the words I've mangled by typing too fast. At one time, you had to go into DOS (disk operating system) and type in your commands in a way the computer would understand; nowadays everybody uses a GUI (graphic user interface) such as Windows. All you have to do is click your mouse button on the icon you want and you will immediately be taken to the program you want to use. You don't have to know which bit of the computer it is stored in or how to command it to start. You just find the right icon and click. How hard can it be?

For those who are interested in learning, there are computer classes freely available all over the place. A beginners' evening class would cost very little and would be quite enough to enable you to do some word processing, compile your own spreadsheet for your household accounts, or compile a database of all your contacts.

KEEPING IN TOUCH

The reason why computers are really valuable to older people is that they make communications over huge distances possible in an instant. For a start, you could use email or instant messaging to keep in touch with friends and family no matter how far away they might live. It is perfectly possible, for example, to chat to someone in Australia in real time. The cost, compared with making phone calls, is negligible, and there is no reason why you shouldn't chat to your far-flung relatives every day if that's what you want.

THE WORLD WIDE WEB

You will often hear the internet referred to as 'the web'. Why? Because it links together millions of computers all over the world and the connection between them can be imagined as a web.

Originally, the idea was to design a system of communications that would survive a nuclear attack. The idea was that if a hole was blown in one part of the system, messages would simply travel by another route.

The internet is a source of endless information. It has on it somewhere the answer to just about anything you need to know – though sometimes finding what you want can involve some persistence. On the internet, you can research and book a holiday, buy aeroplane tickets, or order your groceries and have them sent from the supermarket. You could also investigate your family tree, play games with other people (who may be known to you but who could just as well be living thousands of miles away), or read today's newspaper online and do the crossword. One of the perils of later life is loneliness, but with the internet nobody needs to be totally alone.

FINDING INFORMATION

All web addresses begin with 'http//:'. This stands for 'hypertext transfer protocol', and is simply an agreed language through which different computers and servers can communicate with each other. As the 'http://' prefix is universal, it is often dropped when introducing websites, as in this book (e.g. www.inlandrevenue.gov.uk is actually http//:www.inlandrevenue.gov.uk).

If you don't have a specific address, there is so much information on the web that it is sometimes hard to find just the bit you are looking for. To do this we can use what are called 'search engines'. The most popular is Google, and you will find it at www.google.com (there are many others, but you will soon be able to find those for yourself). If you go on to the Google site you will be able to type in words associated with your enquiry and then press a button to have Google conduct a search of the web using those words. Let's say you wanted to find a holiday apartment in Tuscany. You would type in 'holiday apartment Tuscany' and within seconds the engine will provide you with a whole list of links to possible sites of interest. All you have to do is click on the link and it will take you to the site you have chosen.

Below you will find addresses for a variety of websites, in addition to those in the book, that are of interest to older people. It is only a small selection of what is available, but it should get you started. Once you have the hang of web surfing, you will get used to finding the information you need by yourself.

COMPUTER SUPPORT

Computers made easy (for senior citizens)

This is the site to point your browser at if you feel that you would really like to understand more about computers and what they can do for you. The language is non-technical and there are plenty of useful links to explore. This just might be the site that opens up a whole new world for you.

www.csuchico.edu/~csu/seniors/computing2.html

Support 4 Learning

This is a huge site that contains all sorts of useful information on a mass of topics of interest to older people. The accent is mainly on health matters, but there is also a valuable section on 'silver surfers' with a database of websites that will be of use to the elderly.

www.support4learning.org.uk/health/older.htm

MEDICAL

Medical support

For a wide range of advice on medical matters, try www.netdoctor.co.uk. For advice on all aspects of health you should try the BUPA website at www.bupa.co.uk.

Alliance for Aging Research newsletter

This US site is an absolute *must*. It contains numerous fascinating articles, including 'Shattering the Myths of Old Age'. The newsletter is quarterly and contains nuggets of really interesting information for the older reader.

www.agingresearch.org/living_longer/summer_99/default.cfm

Coping with old age

Here you will find some good advice for those who are not yet old and want to keep old age at bay. Well worth a read. There are some useful links as well.

www.seniors-site.com/coping/old_age.html

The Old Age Metaphysical Country Store

Here is an American site that caters for New Age fans. If you believe you can ease the problems of old age with crystals, pendants and charka bracelets, this is the place for you. It's quite entertaining if you're a sceptic, too.

www.metaphysical-store.com/

The medicalization of old age

This American site considers the role medicine plays in slowing down the ageing process. There are many links to other sites and recommendations for further reading. It is well worth spending some time exploring all the useful information that this site provides.

www.trinity.edu/~mkearl/ger-med.html

Apollo Life

This is a medical site with information about a wide range of conditions. There are numerous articles of interest to older readers.

www.apollo.com

Harvard Health Letter

Again, there is a huge amount of information here that will interest older readers. The site offers the intros to many articles, but should you want to read the whole thing you have to pay $28 and register as a reader.

www.health.harvard.edu

The Department of Health

This is a major UK site dealing with all aspects of health. If you follow the links you can find a large area dealing with the health needs of older people. This is a valuable resource with plenty of useful information.

www.dh.gov.uk

Health and Age

This US ezine offers articles on all aspects of health in old age as well as answering readers' questions. Oh, and there is a button that lets you select a larger font size, even a very large size, to help if your eyesight is not as good as it was.

www.healthandage.com

Shelter Online

Here is a really exciting article for those who aim to keep physically fit as they get older. It's full of inspirational stuff about 75-year-old tennis champions. It's enough to make you get out that old tennis racquet and nip round to the local courts for a quick game.

www.shelterpub.com/_fitness/_weight_training/old_age_muscles.html

SOCIAL

British Council Magazine

This is a wonderful article about a French experiment in which old people and young children were brought together for their mutual benefit. The article is written for the general reader.

www.learnenglish.org.uk/magazine/magazine_home_old_age.html

MetropolisMag

This article on the future of old age is well worth a read. It is written in non-technical language and is packed with interesting info about the hi-tech gadgetry that will make life easier for older people – and we aren't talking about Zimmer frames.

www.metropolismag.com/html/content_1201/mit/

Saga

Saga is best known for its holidays for older people (see page 92), but that is by no means the limit of what they have to offer. A visit to their website is highly recommended for the wealth of interesting information it contains. As well as financial advice for the over fifties there are regular articles on all sorts of subjects including education, living abroad, sex for the older generation and much more. It is well worth a visit, no matter what your interests.

www.saga.co.uk

The Oldie

This is the web presence of the very popular monthly magazine for the over-fifties. It describes itself as 'a haven for fun, good sense and quality writing in a media obsessed with celebrity and "yoof"'. On the site you can find details of forthcoming literary lunches, chat with fellow readers on the message board, or read articles that have previously appeared in the magazine. You can also browse the small ads, buy bargain books or subscribe to 'Webster's weekly email of interesting things'.

www.theoldie.co.uk/

Hell's Geriatrics

This site describes itself as 'for mature folks, and contains a mixture of fun and serious issues. These days "middle age" brings us a new freedom and seniors are rapidly catching up with modern technology. This is your forum, and we welcome your feedback on all topics covered.' The site is presided over by two oldies who rejoice in the pen names Besom and Curmudgeon. There is an email forum that allows you to join in numerous conversations with your fellow members. The tone of the site is humorous and irreverent. Those who like to be politically correct might find that Hell's Geriatrics is not quite the place they were looking for.

www.hellsgeriatrics.co.uk/

Over50s

Over50s describes itself as 'the website for the new generation' and promises that you will find 'information and entertainment tailored for the new generation with features on all kinds of topics from food and travel to legal matters, relationships, finance, health and more. Our focus is on the financial issues that affect you and your lifestyle. In addition there are offers, competitions and prize draws tailored to suit your interests – and as it's your website, we welcome your contributions.' How can you resist?

www.over50s.com/

Senior citizens' website

This is a huge American site that has links to so much information the mind boggles. It is impossible to describe the site adequately, so I suggest you go and take a look for yourself. You are bound to find something of interest.

www.intecon.com/senior/

Third Age

This is an American site with many articles of interest to older readers. The emphasis is on treating older people as if they were actually people rather than patients. It is refreshing to find a site that doesn't immediately try to discuss all the diseases you might die from.

www.thirdage.com/

Old age across cultures and time

This is a really excellent article about cultural attitudes to ageing. It does much to explain the way in which elders, once revered in Western culture, have suffered loss status over the past couple of centuries.

www.trinity.edu/~mkearl/ger-cul.html

Reinventing old age

This is a very good article, originally from *Blueprint Magazine* but reprinted in New Democrats Online. It deals with the impact of old age on the boomer generation. Fascinating stuff.

www.ndol.org/ndol_ci.cfm?contentid=250497&kaid=127&subid=170

Center for Policy Research – women and old age

This US site, part of the University of Syracuse, contains plenty of interesting links and suggestions for further reading. For anyone with an interest in women's issues this is a most valuable resource.

www-cpr.maxwell.syr.edu/gero_ed/family.htm

Woman in old age

This is a very odd site. The content appears to have been written by someone with a very shaky grasp of English, the information is of no real use, and it is hard to see what purpose the site serves. I include it only as an oddity that might offer brief amusement.

members.tripod.com/~sadashivan_nair/
quotwomenquotandrights/id25.html

SCIENCE

Scientific American

This site has many splendid articles that may be of interest. I have picked out one that I particularly liked, but there are links to many others.

www.sciam.com/article.cfm?articleID=00014256-090D-
10EB-890D83414B7F0102

Even In Old Age, Genes Still Influence The Way We Learn, New Study Suggests

This is a fairly heavy read, but it is full of interest. If science is your thing, you'll find this of interest.

www.eurekalert.org/pub_releases/1997-06/NIoA-EIOA-
050697.php

The Royal College of Psychiatrists

This is a huge site full of fascinating information about old-age psychiatry. This is not a site for those who like their information pre-digested, but if you are happy to be challenged by some pretty heavy writing you'll find plenty of useful and interesting information.

www.rcpsych.ac.uk/publications/gaskell/semOAP.htm

The nervous system in old age

If you don't like bad news, you might want to skip this one. It lists all the neurological changes that happen in older people and, to be frank, does not make for comfy reading. If you are the sort who is not easily fazed you might want to give it a go.

faculty.washington.edu/chudler/aging.html

Ohio State University

There is an interesting discussion entitled 'When Does Someone Attain Old Age?' A thought-provoking site with suggestions for further reading.

ohioline.osu.edu/ss-fact/0101.html

New Scientist

This website of the prestigious science magazine has articles on the way in which the mental slowdown of old age might be reversed. Very interesting.

www.newscientist.com/news/news.jsp?id=ns99993686

USA Today

Here's a really intriguing article about hi-tech gadgets and the ageing boomer generation. If you love science and gadgetry, this will keep you entertained and informed.

www.usatoday.com/news/nation/2003-11-16-gadgets-cover_x.htm

Old age appears to be a recent invention

This science site is intended for the general reader, so if you have no scientific knowledge you needn't be put off. This particular article deals with the strange way in which human longevity came about. Fascinating stuff.

www.scienceagogo.com/news/20040606222712data_trunc_sys.shtml

MISCELLANEOUS

On Youth, Old Age, On Life and Death, On Breathing

Here is a chance to consider the views of one of the greatest Greek philosophers, Aristotle. If you enjoy ideas for their own sake then this is the place to go. It gives you much food for thought and a chance to compare the views of antiquity with those of today.

classics.mit.edu/Aristotle/youth_old.1.1.html

Progressive Review – old age

This is a translation of the Roman writer Cato's thoughts on old age. It's not a difficult read and has much that is wise and interesting.

prorev.com/oldage.htm

Old age – what saith the scriptures

This American site is ideal for Christians who are interested in what the Bible has to say about old age. Even if you are not a believer, there is much in this site that may interest and inspire you.

dianedew.com/euthanas.htm

Prince Siddartha encounters old age, sickness and death

Here is a Buddhist view of ageing. There is a lengthy article plus some interesting links. If Eastern philosophy is your thing, you'll find this a useful resource.

alexm.here.ru/mirrors/www.enteract.com/jwalz/Eliade/225.html

The Makeup Gallery

This site is of no real use, but it is quite intriguing all the same. It discusses the way in which movie actors are aged during the course of a story. There are numerous examples with photos showing how well-known actors have been aged.

www.themakeupgallery.info/age/

American Visionary Art Museum

This is a real 'feel good' site for older readers. It deals with the creative aspects of old age and the way in which older artists lead active, useful, productive lives. Even if you've never held a paintbrush in your life, you will find something here to make you feel better about your age.

www.avam.org/exhibitions/blessings.html

Markkula Center for Applied Ethics

Not a jolly read, so if you find the whole issue of suicide too depressing to contemplate just stay well away from this site. If, however, you are interested in such ethical issues you will find a really interesting discussion here.

www.scu.edu/ethics/publications/ethicalperspectives/elder0302.html

Agenet

This is a US site that contains numerous articles of interest to older readers. It covers a wide range of topics including health, drugs, insurance, legal and financial matters, housing and shopping. Although the information is tailored for US readers, there is much that is applicable to all older people.

www.agenet.com

Old-age jokes

Just in case you think we're getting a bit too serious about this ageing business, here is a site that offers plenty of age-related humour.

www.unwind.com/jokes-funnies/oldage.shtml

World Sex Records

The tone of this site is humorous, but it does provide a huge amount of fascinating facts about sex. The subject of sex for the aged is discussed under a variety of headings. For example, the oldest known fertile couple was an 88-year-old black American and his 90-year-old wife. If you like fascinating facts, this is a site that will keep you interested.

www.world-sex-records.com/sex-062.htm

SeniorCentre – old age isn't for sissies

This excellent Canadian site offers a complete course in getting older. And it's free! There are seven lessons in the course and it is all taught via the internet. Although it is aimed primarily at Canadians, everyone else can join in.

www.seniorcentre.ca/docs/studies/aging.html

The future of old age

This is an extract from an American book about ageing. It's well worth reading, and if you like it you can click on a link and go to Amazon, where the book is on sale.

www.energizeinc.com/art/aold.html

Index